Library of Congress Cataloging-in-Publication Data
    Names: Edwards, Braylon, author. | VanHaaren, Tom, author.
    Title: Braylon Edwards : doing it my way : my outspoken life as a Michigan
        Wolverine, NFL receiver, and beyond / Braylon Edwards and
        Tom VanHaaren.
    Description: Chicago, Illinois : Triumph Books LLC, [2019]
    Identifiers: LCCN 2019002922 | ISBN 9781629376431
    Subjects: LCSH: Edwards, Braylon. | Football players—United
        States—Biography. | African American football players—United
        States—Biography.
    Classification: LCC GV939.E38 A3 2019 | DDC 796.332092 [B]—
        dc23 LC record available at https://lccn.loc.gov/2019002922

This book is available in quantity at special discounts for your group or organization. For further information, contact:

Triumph Books LLC
814 North Franklin Street
Chicago, Illinois 60610
(312) 337-0747
www.triumphbooks.com

Printed in U.S.A.
ISBN: 978-1-62937-643-1
Design by Nord Compo
Photos courtesy of AP Images unless otherwise indicated

This book is for anyone in the shadows, the people in the background who put in the work and helped but never got any of the credit.

Contents

Introduction 7

1   The No. 1 Jersey 11

2   A Paternal Bond through Sports 27

3   Mama's Boy 45

4   Playing for Myself 60

5   A Fresh Wolverine 78

6   Breaking Through 92

7   The Rose Bowl and a Big Decision 102

8   The Michigan State Comeback 118

9   Feeling a Draft 128

10   Welcome to Cleveland 138

11   From Romeo to Mangenius 156

12   New York, New York 170

13   Highs and Lows 184

14   The Last Stand. 198

15   A New Path. 216

       Acknowledgments 237

Introduction

NAMES, INSULTS, ASSUMPTIONS—EVERYTHING YOU CAN THINK OF—
I have heard about myself. *Braylon Edwards is out for himself.*
Braylon is about the money. He's a bust, he's a bad guy, he's a
troublemaker, he's a typical wide receiver who doesn't get it. There
are plenty more, but you get the idea. Throughout my 13-year
college and professional career, I heard just about everything
negative that could be said about me.

I've had some pretty great things said about me, too, though,
and I heard those as well. I heard the fans at Michigan cheering
me on, cheering the team on, and 100,000-plus people singing
"The Victors" after wins in The Big House; saw NFL fans wearing my jersey, kids asking for autographs and pictures, and the
smiles on the faces of the fans when we came out with a win
on Sunday, knowing that those people paid their hard-earned
money to come see us play. That always resonated with me and
didn't go unnoticed.

That the outcome of our game could impact their week was
always pretty powerful, too. If we won, that made their week
better; it helped the fans get through to the next Saturday, and
we were heroes. But if we lost, it made their week worse, and as

quickly as we became heroes, we were now the villains. I always felt that weight on my shoulders.

Whether it was positive or negative, the opinions, the reports about me, and what people thought they knew were all formulated by a story that wasn't fully told by me. It was a version of what really happened, but I was never able to tell my unfiltered story on my own. Throughout the course of my life, through the events that played out in public, people believed they knew who I was. I am thankful for the career I had and the opportunity I had to do what I love, but I have always felt this weight on my chest that I never got to tell the whole story. I never dwelled on what other people said about me nor am I asking for anyone's pity. I just want to put it all out there and let people form their opinion of me based on the whole truth.

I've also never fully explained the reason why I loved football so much and made it my career choice. Football is the greatest game there is; no other sport compares to it because you need the entire team to win. In basketball you can have LeBron James on the floor and make it to the playoffs. In hockey you can have Sidney Crosby and Evgeni Malkin flying up and down the ice to get you to the playoffs. But in football if the receiver isn't catching the passes from the quarterback, it won't work. It won't work unless you have a quarterback who can get him the ball. If the offensive line isn't blocking for the running back, you better hope you have Barry Sanders back there taking the handoff, or else it isn't going to work. That team aspect makes football unique and such a different sport. Being part of that team and that unit is something that always drew me to football. I felt like I was a part of something bigger than me. At Michigan my head coach, Lloyd Carr, used to always tell us that it was bigger than us, that the team meant more than the individual, and that represents football in such a perfect way.

That team aspect was important to me because a big part of my life, believe it or not, was trying to find my place. Whether it was with a group of friends, teammates, or family, I have always struggled to find my place. Football helped give me a place and give me a role within that team structure to fill a gap in my life. I was gifted athletically, and it was fun to win—no question about that—but football, and sports in general, meant way more than just a game to me. Going all the way back to my youth, when I trained with my father as a young child, football is a part of who I am. It was how I gained acceptance and made friends in part of my life and it's how I was able to give back to my family and take care of my mom after they did such a great job raising me.

It wasn't easy raising me either. Because I was always looking for acceptance and trying to find where I fit in, a lot of times that meant I was getting into trouble. That's why it always meant a little more to me that the fans, the pundits, and the reporters get the full story from me. The sport meant more than just a paycheck to me; I wasn't just a robot out there playing a game. I'm a human who has dealt with struggles and feels real emotions and I've had a winding path to get to where I am today.

Cleveland is where I really felt that we were seen as robots that had become stats on a fantasy football lineup. I understand that we were entertainers and performers, and that football, especially in the NFL, is a mode of entertainment for the fans. But it was in Cleveland when I thought that we were looked at as gladiators, marched out to do our job. There was no heartbeat behind the padded armor—just a mindless football player running routes.

Writing this book—and just talking about the events in my life—has been very therapeutic, allowing me to get things off my chest and talk about what happened and why it happened, giving people a glimpse of who that person is, that sometimes it wasn't always roses in Ann Arbor. It's about how I felt when I was drafted by the Cleveland Browns, what was going through my head when I was traded to the New York Jets, and also some backstory to my childhood that might help explain some of my fights and legal trouble. From my youth, to high school, college, and the pros, everything has collectively built me into this person.

It has built me into Braylon Edwards, the real person. And while there were some bumps and bruises and unexpected turns, I still wouldn't change the outcome or how it happened. I did it my way and, at the time, I did the best I could.

The No. 1 Jersey

THE NO. 1 JERSEY HAS BECOME A POLARIZING TOPIC LATELY. People have heard my comments and disdain about giving the jersey away and players not earning it, and it has become one of the more misunderstood aspects of my life. They've taken those quotes and made their own assumptions without knowing why I have such a strong opinion on the matter. It's not just about me; it's about who wore it before me and what I had to do to earn that single digit on my chest. I had thought about wearing that number at Michigan since I was a kid, but back then the jersey had to be earned; it wasn't just given away. I asked Lloyd Carr if I could have the No. 1 jersey as an incoming freshman, and he said no. He told me it was a special number and that you had to earn that number, deserve that number, and do right by that number, so I couldn't have it. That's why I wore No. 80 for the first two seasons because I wasn't allowed to get the No. 1. I chose 80 because Jerry Rice was my favorite player, so I wore his number, which was cool and exciting, but the No. 1 was what I wanted.

I asked Coach Carr before my freshman season and then I asked again after spring before my sophomore season started, and he said that jersey number was still to be determined. When he said "to be determined" before that second year, I saw that as hope. There was a chance I could get to wear the No. 1 someday, and I took that as a positive. It drove me to work harder than I ever have.

I wanted that number so bad in part because my dad, Stan, played with Anthony Carter, and all my dad ever talked about when I was growing up was Anthony Carter. *Anthony Carter is the best player in Michigan history. Anthony Carter can run this route, can catch this pass. Anthony Carter, Anthony Carter, Anthony Carter.* If you're a Michigan fan of a certain age or follow Michigan tradition, there is nobody better than Anthony Carter. He was a three-time All-American, finished in the top 10 in the Heisman Trophy voting three times, and played at a time when the passing game wasn't as prolific as it is today. I grew to really appreciate Carter and what he did, and ever since I was a little kid, that number has represented greatness.

In addition to Carter, you look at the names who wore that number and what they represented. David Terrell was given that number as a freshman, played a little bit his freshman year, and then balled out his sophomore year. He was phenomenal as a junior, and then the Chicago Bears drafted him eighth overall. Derrick Alexander wore the No. 1, and people forget that if he doesn't blow out his knee, he might've won the Heisman Trophy over Desmond Howard. Alexander was the No. 1 receiver that year, but he injured his knee, and then Elvis Grbac had no one else to throw the ball to except for Howard, and the rest is history. That's not a knock on Howard at all, but people don't really look at Alexander the way they should.

Those guys weren't the first to get the No. 1, and Carter changed the legacy of what that jersey was and what it represents. What he did was beyond ridiculous and he made that jersey deserve that type of special talent, that selfless player. That number meant so much to me, and I was prepared to do whatever it took to get it. Had Reggie Williams, who was recruited by Michigan as a priority over me, come to Michigan, I know they would have given him the No. 1 jersey. It's not even up for debate because I had this conversation with Williams after we were both drafted.

After we played in the Outback Bowl at the end of my sophomore season, I went and saw Coach Carr two days after we got back from the bowl game. This was before winter conditioning even started, and I wanted the No. 1. I said, "Coach, this is the third time. You told me I had to earn it, I had to deserve it. What do you think?"

He said, "I'll let you know." I also asked him if I could run track, and he said yes to that.

Track was cool because winter conditioning was a bitch, and if I was running track, I only had to do one workout a week. Mike Gittleson and his staff had a goal of trying to make you throw up in winter conditioning. They tried to make you tap out on chin-ups or the ropes. During the ropes session, a trainer would put ropes around you and you had to pull him to you. They did all kinds of stuff to make it difficult, though, like holding onto machines or walking the other way.

If you're super strong, it might only take 12 minutes, but I've seen it last 40 minutes. People got to the point where they would puke or give up. It was at the end of the workout, too. You had already done legs or arms and you're tired and then you had to go to class afterward. That right there at the end of the workout was the devil. Your forearms were already tight, your lower back was tight, and you started to get a headache. I never threw up at Michigan, but there were some times in winter conditioning where I was close.

We got through winter conditioning, and it was time for spring ball. Coach Carr still hadn't said anything about the No. 1 jersey. For the first practice of spring, I went to the locker room and I saw the No. 80 jersey. But I looked closer, and the back said "Matsos." That was Chris Matsos, a walk-on receiver. I went to ask our equipment manager, Jon Falk, what was going on and then I saw it. I saw my nameplate on my locker, and it said "Edwards" with the No. 1 next to it.

I saw it and I started smiling and clapping. That feeling I had was probably, arguably, the best feeling I ever had the whole time I was at Michigan. I did everything they asked of me, kept my head down, and earned that feeling of accomplishment. I was so excited, but a lot came with that number, and a lot happened from the day Coach Carr gave me that number to the Oregon game in September. From March to September, there was a lot that I went through just because I had that number.

I put on the jersey for the first time. It was everything I had dreamed about, and I went up to Coach Carr at practice to say thank you. He looked at me and said, "A lot comes with that number. To much is given, much is expected." From that point on, any little thing I did, he was yelling at me and on my ass. He took a new interest in yelling at me in practice. If he saw me not blocking on the backside, he was yelling at me. If I dropped a pass, which was rare in spring ball, he'd yell at me. He took time to point me out in the meeting if I did something wrong. During a two-minute drill, I dropped a pass that would've been a touchdown to win the practice session, and Coach Carr took the No. 1 from me. I didn't even know he took it from me. This was about a week into spring ball, and I came back, and No. 80 was in my locker.

I wore 80 again for a week and went back to making plays, being quiet, the same stuff I did at the end of my sophomore year, and then I got the No. 1 back. I dialed in and was trying to be the guy I knew they wanted me to be. But Coach Carr was on me for everything. He used to reference my dad and say, "Hey, Stan would get it done." I was like, *cheap motivational tricks aren't going to work on me.*

It pissed him off because after he said that, I told him, "Then go get Stan. Go get Stan and see if he can catch that 9 route." He used to hate that. It's crazy now to think I was talking back to Coach Carr because he is royalty at Michigan. But the funny thing is I wasn't the worst at talking trash to him.

No one talked more trash to Coach Carr than Chris Perry. He said some of the most powerful shit I've ever heard anybody say to Coach Carr. During my freshman year, Perry was a sophomore, and the coaches were trying to figure out if they were going to start Perry or B.J. Askew at running back. When we played Washington, Perry was in the huddle. The coaches sent Askew in for a play, and they told Chris to come out, but he wouldn't come out of the game.

I was in the huddle. We were a in three-wide set, and Chris was like, "I'm not leaving. I'm the running back." Askew was always cool about it, but we had to call a timeout so they could get Chris off the field. That Tuesday after the game, the coaches put Askew as the starting running back on the depth chart. We walked into practice. Chris was looking at the depth chart, walked right by Coach Carr, and said, "Man, this is crazy. If I knew I would've had to deal with this shit, I would've went to Ohio State." We were all shocked. *What did he just say in front of Carr?*

Coach Carr was smooth about it and acted like he didn't hear it, and nothing happened to Chris. He and Carr had a different relationship than I had with him. Had I said that, I would've been kicked off the team, no questions.

I wanted to get that No. 1 back, though, since I was now back to wearing 80. So I was careful about what I said and how far I pushed Coach Carr. I knew they wanted me to stop acting like a clown and do what I needed to do. I finished up strong and got the No. 1 back just by once again putting my head down, being quiet, and doing the right work. I was learning, getting better, and putting in the extra work to really become what that number was supposed to embody. I wanted to live up to what Carter had created with the jersey and all the guys after him, so I did everything I could to put in extra time. But at the same time, I was starting to feel myself again.

When I first got the jersey, Charles, my stepdad, told me to remember that I earned it, that I worked for it and got it, but to make sure I was still part of the team. I remember him saying it, but I let it go in one ear and out the other. Between being recognized on campus and getting the jersey I wanted, I felt like a celebrity. The work I was putting in was starting to show, too. I was killing it in training camp before the season. My freshman year I benched 225 pounds five times. Going into my junior year, I did it 25 times. I was 6'3", 210 pounds. I was fast from running track and strong. We had created a monster.

I was running through training camp and seeing that I was getting better. I was back on track with Coach Carr, and everything was going well except I didn't have a car at this time. I had a car until a drunk driver ran me off the road and into a telephone pole. Pierre Woods, Jacob Stewart, and I were in the car in the winter of 2002, but all of us were fine in the accident. It wasn't serious enough that we got Coach Carr or the university involved.

None of us were injured, we gave the police our information, and they towed our car away.

I didn't have a car now, so I either had to walk or get a ride with someone else wherever we went. I came back to the team hotel after morning practice one day. Roy Manning was my roommate, and I told him I was going to take a nap and to wake me up so I could ride with him to the team meeting. Manning said okay; so we both took naps. The meeting was at 2:00 PM, I woke up at 1:45, and Manning wasn't there. I literally sprinted out of the room with just my socks on, no shoes, down to the lobby. They had a shuttle to take us to the meetings, and luckily there was a bus there. I told the bus driver to go as fast as he could.

We got to Schembechler Hall, and I was hauling ass to get to the meeting room. It was about 1:58, and the meeting started in two minutes. I was almost to the room when I saw Coach Carr's shoulders turn to go into the front door to the meeting room. We had this thing we did for team meetings. When Coach Carr walked into the room, we all went crazy, threw our hats in the air, and screamed and yelled for him. I turned to the other corner to go to the back door and, as I turned around, I heard everyone yelling and going crazy. So I knew I was screwed.

I'd never been late for a meeting. So my plan was to go in the back door and just hang out on the back steps and wait it out. Coach Carr's meetings during training camp weren't very long. He would tell us to have a good morning and then break off into offense and defense groups to meet. When he said, "Let's break into groups," my plan was to get up from the back steps and get lost in the shuffle and pretend like I had been there the whole time. I was sitting on the steps waiting and Erik "Soup" Campbell, my own position coach, ratted me out. He saw me on the steps and told Coach Carr I was over there. Carr saw me and asked if I was late. I told him I just walked in right when he walked in, but Coach Carr used to say, "If you're early, you're on time. If you're on time, you're late, and if you're late, you're forgotten."

He kicked me out of the meeting. He told me I was off the team and sent me back to the hotel. I didn't practice that day or go to any meetings. The next day Coach Carr's assistant called me at 6:00 AM and told me to come down to his office. His secretary, Jennifer, told me that Coach Carr wanted me to sit outside his office. So I sat outside his office by myself with no one talking to me for about 10 hours.

Finally, I left when they told me to go and I headed back to the hotel. The next day Coach Carr saw me and said, "Hey, I don't know who you think you are, but we don't do things like that at Michigan." In my mind, I was four seconds late to a meeting. I didn't have a car, and my ride left without me. I overslept. So that's on me, but I was four seconds late. I had a great spring and summer, was practicing hard, and doing what the No. 1 is supposed to be doing. I never understood and still don't understand why I was kicked off the team, but he put me back on the team and took the No. 1 jersey away again. We were only a little over a week away from the season.

We're prepping for Central Michigan, and on gameday "Soup" Campbell told me I wasn't starting as a punishment. They kicked me off the team, made me sit outside Coach Carr's office for 10 hours, took the No. 1 jersey away, and then benched me. In my mind, I was starting to change into this rebel because why are they treating me like this? He messed with me with No. 80, he messed with me with the No. 1, and if this was someone else, he wouldn't have done the same thing. If this was Dave Baas or Marlin Jackson, would they have been treated the same way? I was comparing myself to other players and I was frustrated. They held true to their word, too. I sat out the first two series against Central Michigan, and then it was me against the world because I was building up this anger and resentment. I caught a 48-yard touchdown in the game and I told myself, *no matter what he wants to do, he can't keep me from shining.* They were about to feel what I can do—no matter what.

I made a first-down gesture in that game, and when I came to the sideline, Coach Carr chewed me out for it. He said, "This is Michigan. We don't do that stuff at Michigan." I caught a one-handed tip pass, and he said, "We don't shine the light on ourselves. That's not how we do things at Michigan."

I finished that game with two touchdowns, but I wasn't talking to Soup or Coach Carr afterward. I wasn't talking to them because they were annoying me. In that game I got my right pinkie stuck in a cornerback's facemask, so I tore a few ligaments in my right pinkie. My pinkie is still permanently bent on its first knuckle because of that injury. They put a splint on it, but it affected the way I was catching the ball because it hurt every time a ball hit it, and then it would reset itself, and the injury wasn't getting better.

During the Oregon game, we were passing a lot because they had a great run defense with Haloti Ngata and a few other guys. Their secondary was awful, though, so Jason Avant had 98 yards, Steve Breaston had around 109, and I had 144 yards. I also had five drops because my finger was messed up. John Navarre had a cannon, so I was trying to body catch a lot of the passes to keep the ball away from my finger, which wasn't working. On fourth down they threw me an in route, and I didn't catch the pass because of my finger. So we lost that game 31–27 because I didn't catch that pass.

After the game, reporter Angelique Chengelis interviewed me, and I told her that I reinjured my pinkie during the game and that I missed a couple passes that I usually catch. She got that answer, went to Coach Carr's postgame press conference, and asked him about it, telling Coach Carr what I said about my finger. Coach Carr told her that he and I weren't on the same page. That was the infamous dustup between us. At this point the whole state of Michigan—and everyone around the country—was thinking I was some type of distraction to the team. Because for him to have said anything, that must mean it's a big deal.

Once again, I didn't start the next game against Indiana. I was livid that I wasn't starting. I was still trying to learn how to catch with this pinkie the way it was, but I still had 144 yards against Oregon. Everybody had a bad game, but I was getting punished again.

We were struggling a little bit against Indiana. Soup looked at me and put me in for a few plays. I caught a 15-yard pass up the middle, ran a post route, and scored a touchdown two plays later. Then they pulled me back out. I was thinking, *Oh, y'all needed a boost. It wasn't working without No. 1 in, and now that we scored, you take me back out.* I was mad, confused, and bitter. But I realized that none of those feelings were going to get me anywhere, so I saw Coach Carr during the week to talk to him about everything and get on the same page.

I sat down and told him he needed to let me know what's going on because I was out there giving everything I had. I told Chengelis I had an injured finger, and he looked at it like I was making excuses. I said, "This thing is hard to catch with." I was here for him, but why do I always have to suffer? I noted that he didn't want me to play, but then when things got tight, I get put in the game. He looked at me and said, "Are you going to get a new finger before the season is over?" I said no. He said, "Then stop making excuses and learn how to catch the ball."

He said that, and I actually thought he had a point. There was nothing I could do about it except work around it and fix the problem, so I manned up and told him we wouldn't have any more problems, and that was it.

The funny thing is my dad had the same exact injury on the same finger. Our pinkie fingers are both permanently bent, so when it happened, I thought it was just destined to happen to me because it happened to my father.

I told Coach Carr we wouldn't have any problems, but I was really looking for something more from him in that meeting. I had a similar relationship with my father. I always was looking for his approval and praise and then I was seeing the same relationship from another man I looked up to—Coach Carr. After two home runs in Little League, there was never a pat on the back. After my high school record in the 200 meters, where was the pat on the back? It was the same thing at Michigan. It was frustrating because all I wanted was a pat on the back, but I was just getting pushback on everything I did.

The good thing for me was that I was prepared for how Coach Carr treated me because of my dad. I was appreciative of my dad's treatment in a way because then I knew I just needed to be quiet and go out and make it happen. That's what I did for the rest of the season. I just made sure that we were together as a team and I was doing what I could to help us win. We stubbed our toe and lost to Iowa, but we rattled off five wins before taking on Ohio State at home. The Buckeyes beat us the year before and they beat us my freshman year, too. They cheated us my sophomore year in the Horseshoe. I scored a touchdown and they called a push-off because Mike Doss, the

Ohio State safety, yelled at the referee. I've never seen home-field advantage like that. It was the latest flag ever. Cornerback Chris Gamble was holding my hand the whole way on a go route. The ball came, I took my hand and pushed it away from his, caught it, and the ref signaled a touchdown. Doss came over all the way from the other side of the field and said, "You going to let that go in our house, ref? You going to call a touchdown in our house, you not going to call nothing?" And the ref pulled out his flag. I couldn't believe it.

This time, though, they were coming into our house. They jumped and danced on our block M in the middle of the field before the game. We saw that as such a big sign of disrespect and used it all as motivation. Ohio State is our rival, and we could knock them off a high pedestal to get to the Rose Bowl.

The night before the game, ESPN Classic was showing the 1997 game when Charles Woodson and David Boston got into a fight. I watched that, and all that was on my mind was fighting Gamble. He got benched for the first drive, so as much as I was trying to get my hands on him, I couldn't yet. He finally got in the game, we got down to the Ohio State red zone, and it was the first time I could get my hands on him and block him. We locked up, and I went after him. I grabbed his facemask and tried to slam him to the ground. He threw a punch at me, and I hit him in the back of the head. The refs broke it up, and I started yelling at Gamble, "All day. I'm going to be on you all day."

On the second play, I cut him. I knew he was ready to throw punches, so I went low and went at his ankles, which pissed him off. We started to roll after that. The coaches started putting me in the slot more. I was usually on the outside, but they played me in the slot so I was away from Gamble and couldn't lock him up. They put Donte Whitner on me, and a guy like that couldn't cover me.

They put me in the slot and called a motion play where I ran an in route. I came out of my break, and Navarre put the ball on me. Nate Salley came down and tried to hit me, but he didn't wrap up, so he bounced off my shoulder, and I took off running. I didn't see anything but the Ohio State band. I scored a 64-yard touchdown, which was the first time I scored on anything over 50 yards in my career.

We ran through Ohio State in that game and won 35–21 in our house. It was my first time beating Ohio State and it was at home. It was the first time we won the Big Ten championship while I was there, so I had the flower in my mouth like Woodson did. I was trying to do the whole Woodson experience because we were headed to the Rose Bowl to play against USC.

That feeling was incredible. I was wearing the No. 1 jersey, we beat Michigan State and Ohio State in the same year, we won the Big Ten, and we're headed to the Rose Bowl. That's everything we talked about before and during the season.

I didn't get into any trouble with Coach Carr or Soup after that meeting with Carr either. I learned how to catch with my pinkie. I kept my head down and worked hard. I didn't feel like they were breathing down my neck anymore after I started changing my mentality. I felt like I was in their good graces finally and I really felt as though the No. 1 was actually my number.

I didn't think it was going to be taken away from me anymore and I understood what it meant to wear that number.

So when I am critical of the Michigan program or Jim Harbaugh for giving it to just anybody, it's not because I'm selfish or I want that number to be associated with me in some way. I think Harbaugh has done some great things at Michigan, and he has made some great decisions since becoming the head coach, but he is a Michigan Man and should understand what that No. 1 means.

I knew what it meant before me and for all the outstanding players that wore it before me, what Carter meant to my dad, what he meant to Michigan fans, and what he created with that No. 1 jersey. And then I went through a battle for two years just to get Coach Carr to tell me I could wear it. I went through a battle after I got the number just to keep it and was put through the gauntlet to make sure I knew what it meant. I was told how important that number was through punishment, discipline, and how high of a standard I was held to.

When I'm critical of that No. 1 jersey, it's because it means so much to me. I have blood, sweat, and tears invested into that number, and if you make someone work for something like that, you can pull out greatness in them. It's not about keeping my name in the spotlight or keeping my name attached to that number. It's about earning something and being part of something bigger than yourself. I also have an endowment for that jersey. I donated $500,000 that pays the scholarship for the player who wears the No. 1 jersey and also for two inner-city kids every year. You can force them to dig deep into who they are and what legacy they want to leave behind with that jersey.

2

A Paternal Bond through Sports

I LOOKED UP TO MY DAD—MUCH LIKE ANY YOUNG BOY. I THOUGHT my dad was Superman. My relationship with him was unique, though, and has changed a lot through the years, depending on what we were going through at the time. I have always looked for his praise and wanted to make him proud. My childhood wasn't what I would consider a stereotypical childhood; I think that's safe to say. That's not just because of how involved I was with sports but because I had a firsthand view of football and athletics through my dad, Stan. He played football for the University of Michigan and was drafted in 1982 by the Houston Oilers. He actually was drafted out of high school by the Baltimore Orioles to play baseball but chose to stick with football and play for Michigan.

He played in the NFL until 1987, and I was born in 1983, so I was around football in some capacity from the time I was a baby to six years old. I was in the locker room in Houston, throwing and kicking the ball around, goofing around in a place that was always very comfortable to me. I was there so much that I was known as "Little Stan" to all the players and everyone around the program.

You typically don't remember much from that age, but those were such great memories that I remember bits and pieces of my time around my dad and his teammates. That's where my love for football started and began to grow. It was all that I knew. My dad and football became synonymous with each other. When I thought of football, I thought of my dad. When I thought of my dad, I thought of football.

Even after he retired from the NFL, we would spend time around the University of Michigan. We would go in the locker room, go on the field at games, and spend time with head coaches Bo Schembechler and Gary Moeller. I was too young to really know what it all meant and how it impacted my father, but I knew that it was something special. I remember very clearly walking out of that Michigan tunnel as a four or five-year-old child, looking around, and thinking this was something monumental. All these people had come to see this for a reason, and it fueled my love for the game.

Even though I grew up around the game, watched it, and studied it, I didn't really start playing football until I was 12 years old. I wanted to play, but my father didn't want to force the sport on me at an early age. He never told me I needed to play and he actually tried to keep me from playing until I was in high school. As is the case when any parent tells their child they can't do something, it naturally made me want to play football even more. I played two-hand touch in the street and threw the ball around with my friends when we lived in Detroit, but it wasn't organized football like I saw my dad and his teammates playing.

At that time in my life, my dad and I were really close. We spent a lot of time together. Even though my parents weren't together, I still saw him on a regular basis. I would spend a week with my dad and then a week with my mom, Malesa. Then I'd spend a weekend with him and some time with her, and we bonded over sports during that time together.

I think most young boys look up to their father, and when you have someone in your life like that, it's important and special to you. So it was difficult when my mother and stepfather, Charles, moved us to Atlanta when I was six years old. I mainly lived with my mom and Charles, who I call Dad, even though he's my stepfather. So when they moved, I was moving with them. That hurt because I wasn't going to be close to my father, which ultimately meant I wasn't going to be as close to football either. As athletic as my dad was, Charles was not. He had to listen to sports talk radio to learn the lingo and sports terminology in order to have those conversations with me. And I love him for that; he spent the time to try to learn about sports just for me.

That helped, but it was just different with my dad and myself. And while football is big in Georgia, baseball was really big in Atlanta. It seemed like everyone there played baseball. So when I came out in the neighborhood looking for some kids to play two-hand touch football in the street, I could never find anyone who wanted to play. It was always baseball, basketball, or kickball, but never football, which made it difficult for me to find my place and fit in.

I think a lot of people have looked at me throughout my career as this boisterous, confident, sometimes cocky wide receiver who thinks the world of himself. But that's really not what was going through my mind, especially at a young age.

Football, and most sports that I played, were the main way that I found my place with friends and classmates throughout my life. For some reason, I just never felt like I was a part of a group. I always kind of felt different or like I didn't quite fit with everyone else. My way of gaining acceptance, making friends, and becoming part of a group was through sports and being the class clown. I thought it would help if people were laughing at what I did, so it led to being the class clown, pulling pranks, or using my smart mouth. At some point, it felt like they were laughing at me and not with me, though, so playing sports was always the main medium where I found my place.

Moving to Atlanta was tough for me because I was leaving Detroit where I had a group of friends I grew up with and where I felt comfortable. When we moved, all the kids in Atlanta in our new neighborhood had grown up together and gone to school together. Now here I came, a kid from the city, and they're all two years older than I. I was athletic and tried to use that to make friends, but it proved to be more difficult than expected.

I had a mouth on me, causing fights after fights in Atlanta. I was the new kid, and it was just like you see in the movies when the new kid comes to town and gets beat up. It felt like I was having a fight a day at some points. Atlanta was really where I learned how to fight because it happened so much. The kids in my neighborhood, for whatever reason, just didn't like me and they made sure I knew it.

We all rode the same bus to school and had the same 300-foot walk from the bus stop to the house, and a lot would happen in that short walk. I was eight and going to Brownsville Elementary School in the second grade. They would beat me up at the bus stop. Everybody in the neighborhood had older brothers, too, so nobody was stepping in to help me; they would only step in to help their brothers. Any friends that I had were on my baseball team, but they all lived in different neighborhoods, so they couldn't help.

At that age that starts to weigh on you, and I was tired of it. So one day I talked to a girl in my neighborhood, who lived a few houses behind me. I told her a plan I had come up with at my house. I watched too many movies, but I had a rubber band with paper clips I was going to shoot at them. I had those metal sticks you use to make kebobs on the grill and a little knife and I put it all in my backpack so I was ready to protect myself the next time it happened.

The girl in my neighborhood told her teacher, who told the principal, and they caught me.

The next day I took the backpack to school, and the principal came into my classroom. The principal asked where I was and where my backpack was. He went into the bookbag and found everything I had put in there. They called my parents, and my mom and Charles had to come get me. They asked me what I was thinking, and I said I'm getting beat up every day and I'm tired of this shit. I said, "You brought me to Atlanta. I didn't ask to be here."

That probably broke my mom's heart to see her son dealing with this, but what could she do? Thankfully, we weren't there for very long and we moved back to Detroit when I was 11. But the process started all over because we were now on the west side of the city, and I was going to Malcolm X Academy where everyone again knows each other. It wasn't as hard, going from Detroit to Atlanta, but it was still hard finding my niche and what I had in common with a lot of the other kids.

We spent two years in that spot and then we moved again, and I was at a different school again with kids, who had been going to the same school, and I had to find my way again. About this time was when I started to use sports to gain acceptance from the other kids. I didn't know what to talk to them about so I'd say, "Hey, let's go race on the playground." We'd race, play basketball, play football, and that's how I got in.

That helped, but I just always felt like the black sheep, no matter where I was. I was trying to find my place with friends and at home and trying to figure out my relationship with my dad and my parents, so I was getting it from both sides. Switching schools so much was only making it worse, and we did it again from sixth to seventh grade when I switched to University of Detroit Jesuit to finish out seventh and eighth grade.

At U of D I was going to school with kids who are white, black, Arabs, Asians. There were all cultures represented there. A lot of them were nerdy, lived in Bloomfield Hills or Farmington Hills. It wasn't Detroit. A lot of kids were taking hikes to get to the school because the education was so good, so none of them lived around me. Sports wasn't interesting to a lot of them, which made it harder for me to find a way to connect. Once I realized the athletic ability wouldn't help me, I went to the class clown role.

If you got in trouble at U of D, you got a JUG, which stands for Justice Under God. I didn't believe God wanted me to write out the preamble because I was bad in class, but I could be wrong. But if you got so many JUGs in one month, you got a Saturday JUG. I got a few Saturday JUGs from trying to make my classmates laugh. You had to come in at 9:00 AM and help out and do whatever. It was like *The Breakfast Club* except I wasn't sitting quiet in the library. I was helping with the groundskeeper or helping to clean the school. It was awful.

That out-of-place feeling continued into high school once I got to Martin Luther King Jr. High, especially because a lot of those kids were from the east side of Detroit, and we were still living on the west side. Those were two different neighborhoods and parts of the city. There were poorer neighborhoods on the east side and a lot of kids without fathers in their lives at the school. They were doing stuff I was not doing. I was not drinking, partying, or smoking. I didn't drink until I was 21 at Michigan, so

I was not really hanging out with a lot of those kids in that crowd and I didn't connect with them.

It has always been a journey for me to find out who I really fit in with, and high school was much of the same. The problem for me was that I tried to change myself so many different times to fit in. I tried to change my personality for what I thought that particular group wanted me to be rather than just being myself and finding the group that fit the real me. I'm a goofball, but I was trying to change my persona in the moment to fit in. So I was looking for acceptance at home from my father, looking for acceptance at school from my friends, and looking for it with my teammates while also trying to earn a college scholarship. Sometimes all of those aspects meshed into one, and that even added to the stress.

Because of my father's success, there were some people around the city who were envious of him. Some of the Little League coaches were made up of guys who played high school football with or against my dad. They didn't go on to play for Michigan or in the NFL, so they were going to punish his son. Baseball and football were both like that. When our travel baseball team played on Belle Isle, our coach always said, "Oh, he thinks he's Stan's son." The same thing happened on the second year of the A team of Little League football, and the coaches there, who also coached at MLK High, said the same thing. I got called up all the time and to run through the drills. They were trying to break me.

Enduring that year after year from a young age coupled with the hard work I was putting in with track, baseball, and football wore on me. It created a little bit of a guarded person who didn't really know who his true self was. This is a side that not a lot of people know about because I never let anyone know that's how

I was really feeling even back then. It was a tough spot to be in and a difficult thing to have go through your mind. I didn't know who really liked me or who was in my corner. Going all the way through high school and having a black sheep mentality helped me create this guarded personality that shows on the outside.

When I was away from my dad and couldn't get my football fix in, I started to really miss that in my life. It was the one constant in my life, the one thing I had been around my whole life when we were in Atlanta. I started watching football even more and studying it, so I could call my dad back home in Detroit and talk to him about the game. At this time football represented my father, so part of that love for the game was my love for him. Knowing what was happening within football kept me close to him when I wasn't able to spend time with him physically. We talked on the phone all the time about football. I remember talking to him about Super Bowl XXV in 1991 as a seven year old, asking him how in the world Scott Norwood missed the field goal for the Buffalo Bills to lose the game by one point.

Another sport that kept us close initially was track. I ran track starting at age nine and I actually loved track more than football. Stan wasn't my coach at that time, though he would coach me later. I traveled back to Michigan in the summer and trained with my coach, Harry Weaver, and then went back to Atlanta for the school year. I wasn't always the biggest kid, but I was always fast, so track was always appealing to me.

When we moved back to Detroit, I continued running track and playing baseball, and that's when the relationship between my father and me started to change. When I said I wanted to play baseball as an 11 year old, Stan said okay. He said we'd hit the batting cages, go to the park to work on fielding, and do base-running drills. I had people working with me, and that's really when our sports relationship started. However, I started to like baseball a little less. I just didn't have the same connection with baseball as I did with football. I liked it and was good at it, but the only fun part about baseball practice was infield fielding and batting practice. The rest is for the birds, and it just never felt the same as running around with a football in my hands.

But my dad was involved in coaching me in baseball, and it was the first taste I got of what him being a coach—instead of just a dad—would look like. He took sports so seriously. I got that feeling with baseball because I still wasn't allowed to play football. I was still playing in the street, though, and now that we were back in Detroit, more kids in the neighborhood wanted to play than in Atlanta. At 11 years old, I was just so much more advanced than the other kids my age. Through running track, being naturally athletic, and studying the game so much, I was just further ahead in most aspects.

When we played around the neighborhood, I got the kids lined up in the huddle and played quarterback. Or if it was a big play, I played receiver and told the quarterback what to do. I could throw the ball a mile, run fast, and was further along than most kids I was playing against.

I stuck with baseball because that's what I was allowed to do, and my dad kept coaching me through that. I was still running track, too. When I was 12, he didn't like the direction of the track program I was with, so we left Weaver and started a new program called Swift with Fermon Tate, a distance trainer who didn't know how to coach sprinters. My dad didn't like that, so he decided he would coach me. That's when I really knew that sports were tough. I realized if I was going to play sports, it was going to be a struggle. I saw the other side of sports as a 12-year-old, and the fun, goofy side of my dad wasn't there anymore.

This wasn't just playing outside with kids and running faster than them. I had no problem beating kids in Michigan in track, but the regionals with kids in Ohio and Junior Olympics were a different story. You're running against kids in Texas, where the heat is the same all year for them, and they're outside running year-round.

We were working out to stay on top and keep me competitive at the highest level. My dad was on it. We weren't doing the workouts that other kids were doing either. My dad is a perfectionist and a stickler, so he was looking at what Michael Johnson was doing for his 400 races, what Maurice Greene was doing for his 100s, and what Carl Lewis and Marion Jones were doing. We were doing Olympic workouts, even though I was just 12 years old. Not to mention, I'm still playing baseball at the same time.

I remember one day I had track practice and a baseball game on the same day. I missed the track practice because I had the game. My mom took me to the game, and then my dad came and picked me up to take me home after the game—or at least I thought I was going home. After the baseball game, he took me to U of D Jesuit middle school and high school for track practice. It's about 6:00 PM, and I had just played a baseball game. It's not the most strenuous sport, but I'm still only 12 and I ran around, hit a home run, a double, and struck out. I played in the outfield, so I'm running around in high grass. This wasn't Comerica Park; this was regular, run-of-the-mill grass. It's fatiguing.

But we went to the track, and he told me how we were going to work out. I looked at my father like, *are you serious? I just had a baseball game.* But he was serious, so I put on my track clothes and got ready. This workout is something that my brothers and I talk about to this day. It's one of the hardest workouts I had. I basically ran eight 200-meter sprints, but the 200s had to be within a certain time, and I only got 30 seconds rest in between each one. As a 12 year old, I was running about 25 seconds and some change for each 200, so he probably gave me about 28 or 29 seconds to run each one. He started the clock, and my only rest time was walking from the finish line to the starting line.

But each time I went around, it took me longer to get back because I was tired. I ran once, got back around, and made the time. I ran another one and got back to the starting line in about 30 seconds. The third one I got back right at 30 seconds, so right when I get to the starting line, the sound to start was going again. After I was finishing the fourth one, I was getting close to the starting line, and he yelled to hurry up. Then I started running to the starting line just to start running again. I took off, and he's yelling at me because he's keeping time.

Then 30 meters from the finish line, I didn't make the time, so I stopped. I bent over and laid down and I just remember him yelling at me, cursing at me. Then he threw a big jug of water toward me. It hit and bounced on the ground before me and splashed everywhere. He told me to get my stuff because we were going. I looked at him like, man, *I just had a baseball game and I gave you four good runs, almost five.* I still had three left to complete the whole workout, but I didn't finish it that day.

By this time it was now dusk. I grabbed my stuff and got in the car. While taking me home, he's yelling that I didn't finish. I didn't live with him, though, so I remember getting out of the car and thinking I didn't need to deal with this. I told my mom what happened, went inside, and wouldn't come out because I was over it.

When we moved back to Detroit from Atlanta, we moved into Green Acres, and my dad moved into Green Acres to be close by. He lived a couple streets over and he measured the distance from the driveway of our house to the driveway of his house, and it was basically the equivalent of running 300 meters. Some days when we didn't feel like going to the track and wanted to get some light work in, we'd run to his house.

He had assistant coaches as spotters that talked to him through walkie-talkies. He'd say, "Go" into the walkie-talkie and start the timer, so I couldn't cheat. That was the beginning of knowing that not only are sports going to be tough at the highest level, but also that this stuff was real. Having a father who was committed to the sport, who had some success, who wants his son to be the best no matter what—it was going to be difficult. That's a tough thing to find out at 12.

He built me, though. He still does it for my younger brothers. He works out my younger brother, Berkley, because my father knows how to create machines. Berkley is a product. We have good genes and DNA and all that, but my dad created Berkley into an athlete.

There's good and bad from that. It was tough to rationalize that young and see the bigger picture that this was going to help bring out my potential. At the time I still equated sports with my father. Any son that has a father around looks for that acceptance. So anything in sports, I was going to go all out as hard as I can, looking for that pat on the butt so I could gain acknowledgment from him.

I started to get tired of just playing baseball at this point. I loved it, but I just wanted to do more and wanted to get into more sports. I wanted to play football, but I still wasn't allowed. I finally begged my dad to play when I was 12. I had to pull in a little help from my stepmom, Carolyn, because she was so sweet, and she had a soft spot for me. She was the only one who could bend my dad's ear, so I would go to her when I wanted him to say yes to something. Usually, it was to go see an action movie or stay out with friends, but this time I told her I was ready to play football and I needed her help to convince my dad. So she convinced him, and he took me up to Tindal Recreation Center on Seven Mile Road in Detroit right by Mumford High School.

The West Side Cougars practiced there and they had already started their practice schedule. They were about four practices in, so it wasn't too late. But in Little League, you started on C team for two years, B team for two years, and then there was A team. Most 12 year olds were on the second year of B team, so these kids had played together for three years. They knew the plays and coaches already. So I was behind in that regard.

My dad went to talk to the coaches, who had heard I was fast. They wanted me to race their fastest guy, Lance Galyard. Everybody called him Lucky, and he ended up playing at Cass Tech and then Central Michigan. Lucky was a big dude. He was like a mutant until he hit high school. Lucky was the same size at Cass Tech as he was in Little League, but he didn't really grow much in high school. He was fast, though, so the coaches wanted him to race me. We're in this thick grass again and we both got on the line to race about 50 yards. I got in my track stance because I've been running track since I was nine. I knew how to get in the blocks, come up, and keep my head down. They yelled go, and I shot out like a bullet. I smoked Lucky, and the coaches knew they had something in me. Lucky was fast. I couldn't beat him when we were about 14 to 16 because he was about 5'10" with big calves, and I was about 5'7", 135 pounds, but I got him that day. They told us to come back tomorrow with my birth certificate and they would get me some pads and equipment.

We went back the next day for practice, and immediately I hated the contact. They tried me at running back because I was so fast. In Little League you don't pass that much, so you put the fast guy at running back. I could always take the handoff because my dad taught me how to take the ball the right way, but I was still learning about the holes. They called 22 Smash. They told me to through the 2-hole or the first hole to the right of the center. So I got the handoff, jab stepped, made the pocket, took the ball, protected it, went into the hole, and got hit so hard that I said never again. That one hit was all it took; I wanted no part of it.

The coach ran it again, and I got hit again. After that practice I said, "Coach, my favorite player is Jerry Rice. Is there any way I can play wide receiver?" The next practice he put me at receiver and started throwing balls to me. I was getting past the corners with ease and catching the ball, so they kept me at wideout.

Because I was fast and could catch, they put me at safety, where I was the last line of defense. Well, I still hated contact and wanted no part of tackling, so I was always about 45 yards back on every play. I was way back watching all the action, and they always yelled at me to get up closer to the play. My plan was: if the running back ever broke loose, I would let him get by me and then I would chase him down from behind and wrap him up because I didn't want to get hit.

I got into fights all the time in fourth and fifth grade at Malcolm X Academy and I never lost fights. But this contact in football was different. I didn't know how to tackle, where to put my head, and how to keep my chin up. And I didn't like any of it. That stinging feeling when you get hit is like when you're playing baseball and you don't have the right grip on the bat. Your hands aren't squeezing the right direction and you get that bad vibration in your arms. That's what it felt like all over.

I didn't like it, but I still wanted that satisfaction of having my dad proud of me, so I finished that season. I went up to the A team the next year, where I had to play against 13 year olds. I hated the contact on the B team, and it was even worse on the A team. They made me play safety again and made me tackle. They'd do these drills that I couldn't stand, too. One was called bull in a ring. One guy stood in the middle, and all the other players made a circle around him. The coach called a number out, and the guy wearing that number ran at the guy in the middle, and they hit each other. We repeated that until the drill was over.

They had another drill where the offense lined up side by side, and the defense lined up side by side opposite the offense. The guy on the end of the offensive line ran behind his line and then turned and ran up the middle alley that was created by the two lines. The defensive player on the opposite side of the line did the same so that the two players were eventually running at each other in this makeshift human alley. I was like, *man this is some bullshit. I didn't sign up for this.*

I was just hoping that my dad was enjoying me finally being a part of the game we loved together. That was how I was going to gain his acceptance. I tried it through academics, but that didn't seem to work too well. The transition you experience from a regular school to U of D's curriculum is something I wasn't prepared for. I don't know that anyone is prepared for how difficult the transition is to the academics and curriculum in seventh and eighth grade. I'm a good student. I've had A's and B's my whole life and made the Dean's List at Michigan.

But in the seventh grade of U of D, I was studying my tail off and I was coming home with 2.8 and 2.9 and 2.7. I was putting in two-and-a-half hours of homework, and it still was not working. It got to the point where I needed to get a tutor just to learn how to study for these tests. I changed things up and I remember getting over a 3.0 my eighth-grade year. I was so proud; I was elated. I took it to my dad, showed him, and he was like, "All right, good job." And I was like, "What? That's all I get?" So I figured to hell with the education; let's go back to football. Because of that reaction, I was not going to flunk out of school or anything, but I knew where I was going to put all my eggs. I had to be great at sports to get that attention from my dad.

So I continued to train and work, even though I was a child. The way it had bonded us had changed, but sports would keep my father and me close to each other. He continued to build me into what he thought I could be and what I should be, and I followed along. We weren't in the locker room kicking the ball around, playing anymore. It was serious, and it became our work, but we were together through football.

3
Mama's Boy

AS MUCH AS IT BECAME WORK WITH MY DAD, IT WAS THE COMPLETE opposite with my mother and stepdad, Charles. When I was with her and Charles, who I also called Dad, it was everything non-sports, which became a great balance for me. I had both worlds; I got to have the athletic side with my father and then also get a chance to be a kid and do regular kid things with my mom and stepdad.

Even when my mom and dad were still together—when I was real young—that's how our relationship was. And my mom was a saint to put up with me when I was real young because I was a menace. She never really punished me or whooped me. She more or less doted on me and just let me do what I wanted so I could have some freedom to express myself. The problem with that was that I had a smart mouth, and I liked to express myself by being a bad kid. To this day, I have a smart mouth, and it still gets me in trouble sometimes—as some of you know already.

When my dad was playing with the Houston Oilers and my parents were still together, my mom and auntie were driving me to a game in Canton, Ohio. I was around three years old and in the backseat of the car, and my mom had just bought me this nice, new outfit that I wore to the game. We were driving in a Mustang convertible with the top down. On the way there, I started taking off pieces of clothing—one at a time—and throwing them out of the convertible. By the time they caught me, I had already thrown out my shirt, my little hat that went with the outfit, my bracelet, and one shoe. When they looked back at me, I was only wearing some shorts and had the other shoe in my hand. All my aunties and uncles always told her, "Oh man, that kid is so bad. You need to beat his butt." But she never did. I was bad around all of them except for my grandma because I always said I'm not messing with the church lady; that's not worth it.

Because my mom didn't whoop me or punish me, I kept acting out. But I didn't disrespect my mother; I was—and still am—a mama's boy. She has always been in my corner even from an early age, and I realized that very early on in my life. I saw this strong, powerful woman in my corner and I adored her. She was my rock.

My dad was cheering for me and wanted me to be successful, and I love him, too, but Mom was the fun one. She bought me He-Man figurines and ice cream, and we went on picnics together. I still love going to the apple orchards and picking apples because of my mother. We went to Arts, Beats & Eats, a festival in Pontiac, Michigan, every year. On Sundays we drove around nice neighborhoods and looked at houses, which became one of my favorite things to do.

At the time, it was just something cool to look at. Eventually, once I was a little older, I realized that it wasn't just looking at big houses. It was my mom and, eventually my stepdad, looking at what they wanted to build for the future. We had everything we needed and had a great childhood, but in their mind, they wanted to be in one of those homes.

They worked hard, so that at some point we could be in one of those nice houses in Grosse Point, West Bloomfield, or wherever. As we drove around, I was taking this all in. When I was about 14 years old, I started planning in my head that I wanted to do something that would help us make that jump. I loved my mother so much and wanted to give back to her because she had already given me so much. We developed a very close relationship off of all those experiences, and she was so patient with me that it brought us even closer. I felt like I could trust her and I abused that trust sometimes, but I trusted her.

When I wasn't out running track or training, I was going to trade shows with my mom. She had a gallery and sold art and jewelry at trade shows. I helped her set up, went on food runs, collected money, and helped close up shop. We traveled together in Atlanta, New Jersey, and Washington, D.C., and that gave me some freedom to just walk around and be a kid. I goofed around and went on stages at the trade shows when I wasn't supposed to. It was helping me be comfortable in a different setting other than athletics and it allowed me to just feel like a kid.

Having that back and forth, the balance between the two parents, was really important for me, especially after my parents separated. My mother met Charles and started dating him very shortly after she and my father separated, and my dad found his new wife, Carolyn, shortly after as well. So I never experienced a time where there was no mom or no dad. No matter what house I was at, there was a mom and a dad, and my dad always lived close to where we lived, so it was never a big deal. I never thought *why aren't we with dad? Why isn't dad here?* Everyone was always close by and a part of our life.

Charles was a big part of the equation for me, too. When he entered my life, I thought highly of him and was comfortable with him almost immediately. He started disciplining me before my mom did, and it actually brought us closer. When I was about four or five years old, I was in the car with Mom and Charles, and something happened where we needed to go back home. My mom had to grab something from home before we went to the next destination, so she went inside, and I jumped in the front seat with Charles. He had some music playing, so I was jumping up and down listening to the music. He told me to sit down, which I did, but I got back up and started jumping again. He said, "Braylon, I said sit down."

So I sat down, but then I stood back up and kicked the off button to turn off the radio. As I did that, Charles slapped the back of my calf on the other leg, and I fell down on the seat. I was in shock that someone whooped me because my mom and dad didn't. I was so appalled that someone slapped my leg, but I thought he was a cool guy, too, so I didn't know how to react.

Then I got scared because I kicked his radio and I didn't want him to tell my mom what I did. But in his mind, he was scared, too, because he just started dating my mom, and if you slap somebody else's kid, that could go the wrong way. So I got in the backseat, looked at him, and said, "Don't tell my mom." He said okay; I know now that we were both relieved.

Oddly enough, that kind of solidified our bond. We had that secret together. He punished me and held me accountable for my actions. I knew to expect it in the future and that I couldn't get away with anything with Charles. I respected that partially because I thought so highly of him. He was always about education and making sure that I had knowledge outside of what I had to learn for school. When we met him, he worked at a hospital. Then he and my mom moved to Atlanta and started a skin care spa. Then when we moved back to Detroit, he was working toward a PhD and going to night school at Wayne State. He became a vice principal and eventually ended up teaching computer applications at Denby High School.

Charles just about seemed to know something about every-thing. I was learning about the Pythagorean theorem in school, and we were talking about it. He recited it like it was nothing, and I was like, *how do you remember that?* I'm young and trying to figure that out, but our conversations always took different forms. I love history, so we talked about Eastern Europe, the Renaissance, Greek mythology, and presidents.

We talked about sports sometimes, too, but just like my mom, he wanted me to see other things outside of sports. He wanted me to hone my intelligence and be able to walk into any room and have a conversation. But when we did talk about sports, he was so supportive of everything I did. Because he wasn't athletic, he didn't have the same expectations that Dad did, so everything I was doing was exciting to him.

If you finished a race in eighth place, he would make you feel like you finished first. Charles always made me feel loved and like I was doing enough. If I struck out in baseball, Stan would say, "You're striking out because your foot is too close to the plate. You need to step off the plate, let the pitch come to you, step into the pitch."

But after that same strikeout, Charles would say, "You had a couple nice cuts. If you would've hit that second one, that would've been a home run." So I was blessed to get both sides. I was pushed, but I also had some encouragement to make me feel good.

I was always a big Sylvester Stallone fan; *Rocky IV* is my favorite movie of all time. If it's on TV, I'll stop what I'm doing and watch it. The David and Goliath aspect of it, the strength and power and training, I just love it. Charles knew that I loved *Rocky*. So when I told him about something I did or what I accomplished, he sang the beat of the *Rocky* theme song. He would start singing real quiet. I'd hear it and I'd keep telling the story, but he'd get louder as the story went on. It got so loud that I would have to tell him to stop, but it was always something I loved. He was proud of me, no matter what I did.

Because he wasn't real athletic, I don't think he really knew how good I was at any given sport. He could tell I was faster than everybody at track, but unless you know the sport, it's hard to really tell how advanced someone is or if the other kids will just catch up eventually. I think the first time Charles really thought I might be a little different was before I started playing organized football at 12.

I was outside our house. Charles got home from work, got out of the car, and asked me to throw him a pass. We lived on Briarcliff Road in Detroit, and our driveway was in the middle of two streets at both ends. There's a telephone wire right by our driveway that runs perpendicular with the street we're on. Charles said to go down the street a little bit, but I told him to go down to the other street where the other kids were standing. He did that, and I went back the opposite way toward the other street. He told me to knock it off and come back and throw the ball, thinking that I couldn't throw it this far. I took one step and launched it, and it went over that telephone wire and dropped right into his chest. Still to this day, we'll be somewhere hanging out with people, and I'll overhear him talking about that pass. That's when he knew I was special.

Once Charles was in our lives, my relationship with my mom didn't change, but the discipline and structure began. As I grew older, they started to get me more in line, but my mom was still my rock. In fact, Charles and my mom both became my escape from sports. It was no longer just my mom; it was the two of them. He was this smooth, cool, laid-back guy. He wore sunglasses, and the breeze just blew through his hair. Mom is like me. She's a hyperactive, strong, type-A personality. Charles is more relaxed. That led to a good balance in my life, and they also balanced out each other in their relationship.

They helped me get through a lot of tough times, especially when I injured my knee in high school. I had Osgood-Schlatter's disease since I was 12 years old. Osgood-Schlatters is a bump on your knee that gets really painful when you're active. It usually happens around the time you have a growth spurt and it's common among young kids who are athletic or train really hard. It was so painful and it would get worse when I ran. It got to the point where I couldn't stand to run anymore.

I used to tell my father that I was in pain, but it would come and go, so it wasn't always there. I don't think he knew how bad it really hurt. We had track practice in University of Detroit's Calihan Hall where the basketball team played. If you went all the way upstairs in the generator room, they had a track up there. The generators were right in the middle of the track, so you couldn't see all the way around to the other side; you could only see one side of the track. The track was rubber, but that's on cement, so you couldn't wear spikes on it.

I was running there when I was a sophomore at Detroit Martin Luther King High School. I was 16 years old, and my knee was just not taking it. I went over to one side and I had to stop. It was hurting that bad. The rest of the kids went around, and my dad didn't see me come around with them. So he thought I was trying to be a punk and wasn't taking things seriously. He didn't understand how painful it actually was and kicked me off Maximum Output's track team. Our relationship took a hit from that. We stopped talking to each other because of it. When we stopped talking, my relationship with my mom developed and grew even stronger. "If he's not going to talk to you," she said, "then I'm going to pick up the slack."

Not long after that happened with my knee, I was playing basketball. I didn't even jump, I was just running on a fast break, and my left knee snapped. I had broken my tibial tubercle. That's what I was complaining about for the last three or four years, and it finally snapped. My mom took me to the hospital, and I had to get surgery on it. My dad found out and realized I was being serious about how bad it was. In my mind, though, it was too late. He should have talked to me about it, and by that time, I wasn't interested in talking to him. It kind of became me, my mom, and Charles versus my dad.

After the surgery I had to have a cast put on, and it went all the way up my thigh. I had crutches, which made it difficult to get around, so the school let me leave class a little early so I could get to my next class. I initially had elevator privileges, but I ruined that by being a dummy. I wrote my initials in the elevator, and the security guard saw it and said, "That wasn't here yesterday before we started letting you use the elevator." I still got out of class early, but after that I had to use the stairs.

King had just installed security cameras throughout the school, and I knew all the security guards there. The head of security was the track coach. I knew the football coach and the dean of students, and the principal at the time was my next-door neighbor, so I knew almost everyone in the school. I got out of my class early one day and was walking down the steps. If you've ever used crutches, you know if one crutch gets too far ahead of the second crutch, you can't catch up. It creates this swinging pendulum affect. So I got the first crutch a step out too far and tried to shift and turn sideways, but I fell down and rolled down the steps.

No one was out of class yet, so I was like, *okay, I'm good; no one saw it.* I got down the steps, went out the door, and walked through the hallway where the security guard was in his booth. What I had forgotten was that they just installed those new cameras, and as I passed by, the security guard without looking up said, "You might want to watch that first step." He caught me.

I had the cast on for about two weeks of school, and then school let out, and I had the cast on for four weeks after we got out for summer break. At 16 I'm going through the rehab process, my father and I still weren't speaking, and my mom said to me, "You know what you need to do." She meant that revenge is the best success. It wasn't revenge against my father, but the goal was to get back stronger and faster.

She was motivating me the whole rehab process because she knew what I wanted to do. She knew I wanted to go to Michigan. I was about to head into my junior season, and it was going to be a crucial year for football to try to get scholarships, so I needed to put in the work. She was right there next to me doing it by my side.

That was a good summer because I got to travel with her a little bit to trade shows, and I was able to get away from track for the first time in a long time. I had run competitively in track from age nine to 15, so this was the first summer I had off. Typically, my year consisted of school, indoor track and basketball (which overlapped), baseball, and then outdoor track. Without any of those sports to play, this was the first time I could be a kid again since I was about nine years old. The only thing I was doing was rehabbing and participating in Jack and Jill of America, Inc, a membership organization dedicated to nurturing future African American leaders through leadership development, volunteer service, and philanthropic giving. It helped kids from all over step outside the box, apply for college, take etiquette classes, etc. A lot of people who had their kids in it were lawyers, judges, elected officials. So that was still fun and allowed me to meet some new people.

It was cool to just relax and get a taste of what it was like to just be a kid again. Rehab went well, and I got through my junior season. I had good grades throughout high school, but I got bored easily, so I started figuring out which classes I could skip. I didn't skip all day except the fifth and sixth period and I was getting A's in those classes anyway. I started hanging out with a couple of cats who were into that. Nobody was selling drugs or doing drugs or anything like that, just skipping some classes.

Our school was in downtown Detroit, so you could jump in a car and hit Greektown and go get some food at Niki's. If you had some money, you could get pizza at Pizzapapalis. Belle Isle was also right there, so we skipped one day, went to Wendy's, got some nuggets, and then went to Belle Isle. Some girls skipped, too, and we were out sitting by the fountain when some cops saw us. The cop came up and asked for a school schedule, which was on our school IDs. If you're off and don't have class at that time, then they won't trip. But if you're supposed to be in school, they have to report you and take you back. I didn't even have my ID on me, the girls were a year younger than us, and they had class. The guys we were with had class, so they took us back to the dean of students, who then called my mom.

I get home, and my mom just couldn't believe that I was skipping class. I explained that I had a 3.6 average and just went to get some chicken nuggets. I left a class where I got an A and I was just hanging out. I didn't think it was all that terrible. She was upset, though, and she told me I needed to go stay with my dad. My dad only lived about a 25-second run away, but this was right before Christmas break.

It was winter in Detroit and freezing cold outside. I knocked on my dad's door, and he said I couldn't stay there. He said he didn't want kids there who were skipping school and messing around. I was like, "you don't even know what I do. When's the last time you asked for a report card?" He said no. Plus, on top of that, he had my brother, Berkley, who would've been four at the time, and Bailey, who would have been one. My dad also adopted his younger brother and sister because my grandfather was a rolling stone, and the kids needs needed to be taken care of.

So I was kicked out of one house but couldn't stay in the other. It was cold, and I needed to go somewhere, so I went to my friend Brent's house. He lived right behind my mom's house, and since both parents thought I was at the other's house, we went out that night. We went to a teenage party, went bowling. I was living it up.

But by the end of the night, Brent's parents said I couldn't stay at their house. By that time it was late, getting even colder, and I had no place to sleep. I decided to go back to my mom's house. I got in the garage, and she had one of those Ford SUVs with the numerical code on the door handle to unlock the door. Somehow I remembered her code, got in her car, put the seats all the way down, and slept in the garage. There was no heat, but I slept there all night.

In the morning my mom woke up, came out to the garage to go somewhere, and saw me sleeping in her car. She freaked out, asked me what was going on, and took me in the house. I told her my dad said I couldn't stay there. So once again this becomes me and my mom versus my dad. I also managed to dodge punishment, which was great because Christmas vacation was coming up. Now she felt bad, and I was able to sell it and play it up.

Up until that point, my father and I had communicated a little bit through the football season. But once he said I couldn't stay at his house, we once again stopped talking to each other altogether. It's important to say, too, that when I say it became "us versus him" that my mom never put him down or talked down on him to me. She would always tell me that my father loved me, we had a different relationship, and that he'd come around eventually. She always talked him up.

Each time my dad and I stopped talking, it was like a piece of me was missing. It didn't matter how loving and accepting Charles was. It was my dad, and you want that acceptance from your dad. If I didn't have my mom there to support me, I think this story would be a whole lot different and I would be a completely different person. As it had been with everything else in my life, I needed everyone in my family to be able to get to where I wanted to go, but as I got older, I started to realize that a lot of my fate rested in my own hands.

4

Playing for Myself

BEFORE I TURNED 12, I WANTED TO PLAY FOOTBALL SO BAD because of my father. Then once I actually started playing organized ball, I realized I hated contact and really wasn't having that much fun with it. I wrestled with it mentally because I had built it up so much in my head, but once I took that first hit on the West Side Cougars team, it was like that tackle jarred me to what the reality of it all meant. Then it wasn't just fun and games for me. It wasn't until I was 14 that I really began to enjoy football. But even then, it still wasn't what I wanted it to be. Looking back on it, I think it was because I still wasn't doing it for myself. I was still doing it for my father.

I played Little League my freshman year for the A team of the West Side Cubs, and that season was where I started to let loose a little bit. We were able to compete and were winning some games, though we lost in the semifinals of the playoffs to the West Side Bucks. I was playing wide receiver now, too, which helped because that's the position I really wanted to play. One of the coaches on the team, Reginald Hinton, played at Western Michigan and was a really good player for them in the 1980s. He and my dad set it up before my freshman season started that Hinton and I would run routes on Sundays. I was only 14 at the time, but I was ahead of the curve. Now kids are learning routes, ladders, cone drills at 12 because the game is so accelerated. But back then, we were doing stuff that no one else my age was really working on.

Through working with Coach Hinton, I felt like I was improving and getting better at my position. I got through that freshman season and really didn't do much my sophomore season at Martin Luther King Jr. High. After that second season, I broke my leg, and me and my father weren't speaking. I got through the rehab process, the summer was over, and I told my rehab therapist that I was ready. I had full extension in my knee, was bending it, and working out on it. Even though I wasn't 100 percent, it was about to be my junior season, and I knew I needed to get back.

King had been practicing for a week already, but I had talked to the coaches about my injury and that I would be out there once I was ready. I had been running in the pool, jumping in the hallway. I was like Cuba Gooding Jr. in *Men of Honor*, just grinding it out. It hurt really bad, but I was determined to get on that field and do something.

I had put in work since I was a nine-year-old kid on that track field, on that baseball field, and eventually on the football field. I had walked through that Michigan tunnel and onto that field with my father countless times, and my dream was to play on that same field one day. Up to this point, though, I hadn't done anything to garner any interest and now I was coming off of an injury, so things were looking pretty bleak for me.

My mother and father both knew that Michigan was the goal, and my mother reminded me of that throughout the rehab process, that I needed to get back if I was going to earn a scholarship. So this is when football started to change for me in terms of how I viewed it. It was the beginning of me playing for myself and not for my father.

I wanted to earn this scholarship and I still wanted to play for the same school my dad played for and follow in his footsteps, but I wanted to earn it myself and get a different form of acceptance. I started playing football for the acceptance of my father, but earning a scholarship would mean that an outside voice approved of what I had done, and that became important to me.

It was funny. That first practice I attended of my junior year was like the first day of Little League all over again. They wanted to see how fast I was, but this time they wanted to make sure I was fully recovered from my injury as well. Instead of a race, they put me in one-on-ones against a defensive back. He was fast and was going into his senior season. He wasn't on the track team, but he should've been. They wanted to see me run a route and make sure I could go.

The quarterback gave me the route, which was a simple post route. But everyone was waiting to see if I could plant on my injured left leg and turn up field or if it would buckle. The corner played off coverage, and I just remembered everything Hinton taught me on those Sundays. The key was to make everything look like a go route and run straight lines. I ran at the corner, and he opened up to cover a go. I put my left foot in the ground, made a perfect cut, went inside, and the quarterback threw the ball. I caught it for a touchdown. The coaches all looked at each other and said, "Yeah, he's ready."

That information that I was recovered and that I was ready to play this season, of course, made its way back to my dad's house. So now, all of the sudden, he came back in my life, and we were talking again. I was still upset, but I wanted him in my life. He got me cleats, gloves, and all the equipment I needed for the season. Because of what I was doing on the field, everyone thought my leg was fine. I, though, was really the only one who knew that my knee wasn't right. My doctors had signed off on it, but I was the only one who knew there was any pain. I had dealt with much worse pain through my Osgood-Schlatter's. So as long as nothing broke or popped, I would make it, but it still limited me in what I could do. It wasn't right the whole season, and my knee was killing me after each practice.

Because of the pain, I was struggling on the field, and it made me look like I was not a good football player. At this point I was only playing receiver because I still didn't like tackling. The King coaches put me at defensive back for my sophomore year. We played against Mumford, and Mumford had a big running back at the time. He was built like T.J. Duckett, who played at Michigan State. This guy got a sweep, the receiver tried to run me off, but I saw what was going on. I tried to come up on that running back, and he just flat ran me over. I got up and thought, *this is why I don't like hitting.*

I made it through my junior season, but I felt like it was kind of a wasted year on the field. I wasn't fully injured, so I didn't really have an excuse, but there wasn't anything on my film that would make any college coaches jump out of their seat and offer me a scholarship. But I was able to take a little positive out of our last game of the season.

We went to the city championships, lost against Henry Ford High, and then lost to Eisenhower High in the playoffs. They had the DiGiorgio brothers on their team, and John, who played line-backer, was a tackling machine. He was always in the paper with like 20 tackles a game. He was all over the place. Even though we lost that game, I found some confidence in what I could do on the field. I had nine catches for about 130 yards. I didn't score, but I was open the whole game and I caught everything. So because of my performance, I thought maybe I can do this. Despite the season I had, maybe something special could still happen for me.

After the season was over, I wanted my knee to fully heal, so I didn't do indoor track that year. That was the second season of track I missed because of my knee, but I thought it was the right decision given how hard I had worked my knee during the football season. After Christmas break of my junior academic year, my mom picked me up and asked me how my first day back was. I said it was fine, and she said, "Good, this is going to be your last day at King."

The next day they enrolled me at Bishop Gallagher High. Just like when I was younger and we moved to Atlanta from Detroit and then back to Detroit from Atlanta, I was switching schools again and trying to make new friends. This all happened because my dad had been talking to Darnell Hood, who played football for Bishop Gallagher but also trained for track under my dad. Hood was a year younger than I and he actually wound up going to Michigan, too. But he told my dad that he had a great experience up to that point at Bishop Gallagher, and that the head coach, George Sahadi, knew what he was doing. I guess they had been talking all along without me knowing, trying to get me in there because my dad wasn't happy with how everything played out at King on the field.

So they transferred me to Bishop Gallagher, and I went from this big school in Detroit to a little hole in the wall, Catholic school with 400 kids total in Harper Woods. I was the biggest kid in the school. There was one other kid who was taller than I, but he wasn't athletic. By this time, I was about to 6'2", a big step up from the little 5'7" kid who started high school at King. Part of why I broke my leg and had Osgood-Schlatters was because I grew six inches in around three months my sophomore year. I came into my own around this time. I had a little facial hair and waves in my hair. I was always worried I was going to be ugly, but I had come into my looks. I was 16, about to be 17, had a little confidence in myself, and was the big dog at this new place.

I got to Gallagher and met with Coach Sahadi, and he was like this happy grandfather figure. He was a heavier dude, so he always had snacks in his office. You could always go back to his office and kick it with him, and he was always understanding if you had a problem and he always had your back if you had his. My first impression of the school and the football coach was very positive. I knew Hood through my dad and then I also met my best friend, Justin Jarvis, very early on once I transferred.

I built off of the confidence I got in my last game against Eisenhower and now I had some positivity going at Gallagher, so things were starting to roll in the right direction for me. The only negative was that in Michigan, when you transfer schools like I did, you had to sit out athletics for half of a semester, so I couldn't run track or play basketball. The first time any of the students or coaches really got to see me in action was at a volley-ball tournament the school put on for March Madness. I was on a team with some of the other juniors and I was all over the court, spiking it, blocking people. In between games I was playing around and dunking the ball. People were looking around like, *are you seeing this? This kid is ridiculous.*

I wasn't focused on many sports, but luckily I found a bal-ance—similar to how I did with both my dads. I had an English class with Mr. Strong and I absolutely fell in love with his class. I fell in love with Shakespeare when he started teaching it. I have always been into kings and queens and the Renaissance era, but the way he taught it was special. It was with so much passion and so much fun.

I got good grades in school, but I was the type of person who did my homework in class and then dozed off. Somewhere around the 20 or 30-minute mark in class, I was the one with the hat down over my eyes. But in his class, I could read, give input, and was engaged. I had always been attracted to Shakespeare's work, especially *Hamlet* and *Macbeth*. It felt like Mr. Strong was a Shakespeare character, like an old general who had been loyal to Hamlet for years. He was a cool dude, but you couldn't play around with him. He would kick you out and give you detention if you acted out, but he kept it so interesting that I never had any issues in his class.

It just seemed easier at Bishop Gallagher. Life was good, I was this larger-than-life character there. The 40 girls who went there were trying to figure me out, and I was trying to figure them out. I was having fun, but I was also missing the athletic side of my life. I was sitting out because of the transfer, and, coincidentally, my father and I still weren't talking. I didn't have sports in a literal or metaphorical sense.

At the end of March, Coach Sahadi started telling me about a football camp in Canada. It was being held at the University of Windsor and it was for kids in Canada to get exposure to scouts and coaches who came to the camp. Those prospects wouldn't have had the chance to get in front of any American coaches if it had not been for that camp.

I wasn't doing track, baseball, or basketball, so I had just been training on my own. I was just running around the neighborhood. After waking up, I'd run two miles. I'd do sprints down the side streets. I had been running track since I was nine. So by the time I was 17, I pretty much knew what I was doing, but it wasn't the same as really participating and staying in shape. But I decided to go to the camp Coach Sahadi suggested. I thought it would be a good opportunity for me, especially since I had some confidence off of that last game, and my knee was finally feeling better. I was in a great place mentally and felt as if this could be a big step.

My mom drove me from Detroit to Windsor, and from start to finish at this camp, I put on a show. At football camps, when the quarterbacks find receivers who are really good or receivers they like throwing to, they'll line up to make sure they get reps with that guy. That's what the quarterbacks were all trying to do with me. I was running post routes, slants, go routes, and my knee was feeling great. I was bigger, stronger, faster. I was just killing dudes out there.

I ran the 40 at the camp and I ran a 4.58 and a 4.6 flat at 6'2", 190 pounds and 17 years old. After that camp that's when I started getting recruiting letters from coaches. Michigan, UCLA, and Wisconsin all started writing me letters, and Cal, Vanderbilt, and Michigan State all got in the picture. Now things were starting to pick up on the football field, and it looked as though I might have a realistic shot at accomplishing my goal to someday play at Michigan.

Not only was I talking to Michigan now because of the camp, but Coach Sahadi also had somewhat of a pipeline to Michigan as well. Julius Curry was older than us, but he went to Michigan. His brother, Markus Curry, was about to go to Michigan when I first got to Gallagher, and Lloyd Carr had a connection with Coach Sahadi. And, of course, my dad went to Michigan, too. All the lines were connected. I just needed to show the coaches what I could do.

Michigan's camp was usually held in the early summer around the end of May or early June. Before the Michigan camp, my dad found out about my performance in Windsor and wanted to help me prepare for Michigan's camp because it was going to be a whole different beast. This was a multiple-day camp, and it could be my only shot to earn a scholarship.

We didn't talk from about December to May, but he came back and had me come out to track practice before the Michigan camp. We were pulling the sled, running, doing our thing because I hadn't really done anything in football for the first three years in high school. So this performance was going to be crucial to show my potential. We trained all the way up to the camp to get me ready. My parents dropped me off at the camp, and from the get-go, it was over. I was running routes and just torching cats. They had the smokehouse, which was a competition in the 40. The fastest 40 times raced against each other, and I got second overall. I ran a 4.49 at this camp after training for a little less than a month with my dad. The guy who beat me was beyond ridiculous. He ran a 4.4 flat, but I got second overall. Then I won the hands competition. They kept turning the speed up on the JUGS machine to see who could catch it the cleanest. If you double caught the ball, it didn't count. So I had some confidence, a little swag going.

My dad wasn't up there the first day, but he came up one of the next days to watch the camp. It was funny because my dad knew all the coaches at Michigan, so when he got up there, they started yelling at him, asking if he was hiding me from them on purpose. Jim Hermann, who my dad knew from his playing days, cornered him and asked him if he had something against them. But they didn't know the whole story, that I really didn't go to any other camps, that I transferred, and that I broke my knee. Anyway, they were upset with him.

Despite all of that—the second-place finish in the 40, the hands competition, putting on a show in one-on-ones—I walked away from the camp without an offer from Michigan. I was disappointed, but I still had a lot of fun at the camp. It was the first time where I felt like I was able to showcase my potential but still understood that I really didn't have any film to go with that performance. During the season I would have to show the coaches what I was capable of.

At the same time, though, I also couldn't sit around and wait for Michigan. It wasn't an all-or-nothing type of deal. If Michigan didn't offer me, I still was going to play college football. I wanted to play at a high level. So after the Michigan camp, I went and participated in Michigan State's one-day camp in East Lansing. This was about a week after the Michigan camp, and I did the same thing at Michigan State that I did at Michigan. The difference was Michigan State head coach Bobby Williams pulled me and my dad into his office and offered me a scholarship on the spot. That was the first big school to offer me, so I couldn't believe it.

I had already been offered by Akron, which was my first scholarship offer and something I was excited about. When I got the Akron offer, I thought about the road I had at King—the injury and everything I had done—and I was proud of myself. But this was the Big Ten. The Michigan State offer was a big deal. To see that offer come through was an amazing thing because it meant that it wasn't really a dream anymore. It was something that I had in my hands and could actually move forward with. But at the same time, it was a little frustrating that Michigan State offered at their camp, and Michigan didn't. Michigan State didn't have any film, but the coaches saw the stock I came from with

Stan Edwards and that I was skilled with size, speed, and tons of potential.

What happened was Michigan had Hermann recruiting the Catholic schools in the area, so he recruited Bishop Gallagher for Coach Carr. Hermann is the reason I almost went to Michigan State. That was when Charles Rogers was there. Could you imagine us playing together? That would've been nasty. I went through the rest of the summer and I didn't really have any communication with Hermann. The season hadn't started yet, though, so I wasn't worried at this point. My knee kept getting stronger, I was running track again with my dad, I was on pace to get to where I wanted, I was getting my confidence back, and I was feeling good about the direction we were headed.

Going into that senior season, we had a really good quarterback, Sam Martinisi, returning. I was excited about the potential, but before our senior season, he got hurt. Our backup quarterback was a freshman from Berkley named Brian Seery. He was young, looked like Charlie Conway from the *Mighty Ducks* movies, and did what he could during the season.

We started out beating the hell out of Divine Child High at the Pontiac Silverdome 28–0. That was the same place where I had thrown all my clothes out the window to see my father play, and now I was there winning my own games.

This Gallagher team was something incredible, too. It was a small school, so we didn't have a starting offense and a starting defense. We had maybe 35 guys total on the team, ragtag kids, playing both ways. I broke a state record that year for positions started because we didn't have the bodies and because I was so athletic. I started at kicker, punter, long snapper, kick returner, punt returner, wide receiver, running back, quarterback, defensive end, linebacker, corner, and safety. It was ironman football.

That season was when I really loved football for myself, too. I had earned the scholarships and put in the work. I was starting to really have fun with football because I was doing it for me instead of for someone else. The problem was I still didn't like hitting when I got there. I realized once I got to Gallagher, though, that a big part of that was because I didn't know how to hit. Coach Sahadi actually taught me how to tackle. Now that I was bigger, faster, stronger, and knew how to hit, it was a completely different ballgame for me. I was no longer the nail; I was the hammer.

I was 6'2", 190 pounds with 4.4 speed, which is a lot of force coming at you. So Coach Sahadi had me play safety because I could do a little bit of everything. I figured out that I could run up to people full speed and if I caught them in full speed I could do some real damage.

We beat Divine Child and lost to De La Salle Collegiate High, but in that De La Salle game, I had about 11 tackles, an interception, a touchdown, and 100 yards returning kicks and punts. My stats and my film were starting to get to where I needed it to be despite not having our starting quarterback.

Charles was at that Divine Child game. I was playing safety, and the running back took a sweep to the left. I read it and just ran like a torpedo and hit him so hard. He flew back; I flew back. He dropped so hard that they thought he was knocked out. I rode home with my mom and Charles after that game, and Charles just looked at me with eyes wide and said, "Man, when did you start hitting like that?"

With my dad it was business. Dad was in the stands with the stopwatch saying, "Not bad, not bad." That was his way of saying good job. With Charles it was like I was Benny "The Jet" Rodriguez from *The Sandlot* lacing up the P.F. Flyers and wrangling the beast. It was fun to talk to them both for different reasons. Dad could see the growth at the position, and he would say, "I liked how you set him up on that route." That made me feel good because he knew I was studying, and I knew he was watching. Charles was just so excited to see it. It was like a kid on the playground. He was the guy in the stands after a big play, saying, "Did you guys see that? That guy right there, that's my son, Braylon Edwards. I'm Charles, his stepfather." That felt good, too.

I was doing a lot of that on defense, though, because Martinisi was still out, but he finally came back for the sixth game of the season against Riverview Gabriel Richard. The first play of the game was a 70-yard touchdown. We ran a slow post, and I was so excited we were about to show them what we could do. Our defense then made a stop, and we got the ball back. We ran a go route, and Martinisi hung the ball up, and I had to come back and get it. The second play of the game, I looked back, and Martinisi partially tore his ACL. I couldn't believe it. I thought we had our quarterback for the last part of the season and I'd have a chance to really shine on offense, and then he got hurt for a second time. We made the playoffs, but we would've gone a lot further if we had our starting quarterback the whole year.

I had some offers under my belt. Since I was showing my athleticism in other ways on the field, some bigger schools started coming after me. School was going well, my dad was happy, and he was the cheerleader of the year that season. My mom was happy because she could see that I was happy. But Michigan still hadn't offered, and that was weighing on everyone. I had been to Michigan since I was four years old. I had been to Michigan games throughout that season with my dad but still had no offer. I hadn't had much communication with Hermann, so I was thinking there's no interest.

Meanwhile, Vanderbilt, Cal, and Michigan State started to be the front three. Rock Banton, who was a Bishop Gallagher great, played at Vanderbilt. So he was pushing hard for the Commodores. I had the coach calling me at school; they're even pulling me out of class. The head coach at Vanderbilt was telling me about a quarterback they had coming in the class after me. They said he's going to be a first-round draft pick. That quarterback was Jay Cutler.

Michigan State said I could wear whatever number I wanted. We're in the number-talking phase, that's how serious it was. Michigan State said when Charles Rogers left, I could have his No. 1, but they would get me a cool number until then. Cal was trying to sell me on the weather. Jeff Tedford was a quarterback guru out there, and little did I know that I would have been catching passes from Aaron Rodgers.

These schools were showing me a lot of love, so it was at the point where I was thinking Michigan wasn't valuing my skills and my abilities. That was fine. I didn't have to go to Michigan. That's where my father went, and that would've been cool, but I didn't have to go there to become what I want to be. I could start my own legacy. I've been going into that locker room at Michigan, singing "The Victors" since I was born. I've been going to spring ball, hanging on the sidelines. They know my dad. They know my family. But it's like I wasn't good enough for them. My parents expressed their concern about the lack of communication and interest in me.

Then Erik "Soup" Campbell took over my recruitment from Hermann, and it became completely different. Soup was in constant contact, telling me that Michigan wanted me, but he just needed some time to get everything back in order with my recruitment. I was invited to come out to the Wisconsin game during the 2000 season, so my dad and I went to take in the game. Michigan won that game 13–10 against a ranked Wisconsin team, and I think I might have caught Coach Carr in an emotional moment after the game. Coach Carr came in the locker room excited and ecstatic. Back then, the football locker room was connected to the basketball locker room.

They kept the recruits in the basketball locker room, waiting for Coach Carr to give his speech to the team. But this time he locked eyes with me as he went into the locker room and he came straight over to me. He looked at me and said, "Hey, do you want to go to the University of Michigan?" I was like, "Hell, yeah, I've been here. What have you been waiting for?"

All the stuff I had been talking about—I don't need Michigan, I can go elsewhere, forget Michigan—all went immediately out the window. My dad was there with me when I was offered and even he was at a loss for words. After all the work we put in, the day had come for him that I would be able to play in The Big House just like he did. The journey was a long one, but we did it. I called my mom as soon as possible on my dad's cell phone. She was jumping for joy, going crazy, yelling. I got back to her house, and she jumped up and hugged me. She said, "We did it. You did it. You stayed the course and you did it."

That was exactly how it felt. I did it. I put in all that work, went through all that strife from a little nine-year-old kid running track to a 12 year old getting water jugs thrown at him, breaking my knee, rehabbing it back. Football now meant more to me than just my dad. Football was something I had invested in and saw the reward of all the work I put in. I had accomplished something spectacular. I committed to Michigan shortly after that and was locked and loaded from that point on. I never took any other recruiting visits or entertained any other schools. Michigan was it for me.

A Fresh Wolverine

YOU CAN'T START WORKING OUT FOR A COLLEGIATE TEAM UNTIL you graduate high school. So I didn't start working out at Michigan until I graduated on May 20. The reason I remember that date is because it's my dad's birthday. Once I graduated I was pretty much running track for my dad and then working out in Ann Arbor. Whatever free time I had in Ann Arbor was spent doing 7-on-7's, lifting weights, watching film, and getting the lay of the land. It was a busy time in the physical world for me, trying to switch from lifting high school weights to a college lifting program while running track at the same time. That was a lot.

It was a big adjustment from a weight perspective. I was working out with Mike Gittleson, who was Michigan's strength and conditioning coach at the time. Gittleson was a Vietnam War vet and was the strength coach when my dad was at Michigan. He was an animal in terms of what he expected out of us, and it's a different breed going up there pulling ropes, carrying sand bags 100 yards and back, doing chin-up workouts. It was intense. The good thing for me was that I had come to expect hard workouts. Because of my dad's training regimen, it didn't really bother me to work that hard in the weight room. It was still an adjustment and difficult, but I almost expected that because of how I was raised.

I got through those initial workouts, finished track, and then training camp started at the end of July. This was when they still had regular two-a-days. They did freshman two-a-days first, so that as an 18-year-old guy fresh out of high school, you could get used to what that type of practice was. So we had three or four days of freshman two-a-days. We had a full padded practice in the morning, got lunch, watched film, talked about the morning, and then went out and put the pads on and did it again in the early evening.

We stayed in the dorms at this time, so we didn't have the hotel with the comfortable beds or air-conditioned rooms. We had small beds, and sometimes you had to catch a bus or walk early all the way down to Schembechler Hall to make it on time. But those first few days taught us how to get into a rhythm and figure out how your day was going to go.

On the third day, the veterans came in. So now we had first team, second team, and third teams, and I was trying to make my mark. That's when I noticed the biggest difference from high school to college. The speed of the game was so much different. I did well in 7-on-7's in the summer, but once those pads were on, everything was different.

But because I had trained so hard in the offseason after graduation, I felt like I was in the best shape of anyone, including the veteran guys. The veterans worked out in the summer at Michigan, and then they got a little break before the season starts to do whatever. While those guys were out and about, relaxing, I was still in AAU track season. We were traveling for regionals, states, and the Junior Olympics in Virginia. As soon as the Junior Olympics were over, I had about a week before training camp. So I was in tip-top shape, and that was something I was appreciative of about my dad. Guys were out there dying at training camp. It was a hot summer that year, but I was able to go. I had wind.

If you're trying to get a job, trying to beat out veterans, you have to be able to show you can handle it. If Erik Campbell, our wide receivers coach, called your name, you had to get in there. He talked with a lisp so he'd say, "Hey, uh, ith your turn 80, get in there." I was ready to go, as opposed to Tim Massaquoi, who was a wide receiver when he came in. He was a little tired, and when you're young, you don't have the skillset to rely on when you're fatigued. So the little bit of skill you have goes out the window, and you're going to look bad on film.

Because I had been around the players and the school so much, once I put on that Michigan T-shirt and those shorts, I felt like I fit in with everybody. I had some confidence from my senior year and I honestly felt like everyone had a clean slate now that we were all on the same field. It didn't matter who had five stars and who had four stars because we were all trying to earn a spot now. The big thing for me was trying to prove I belonged and trying to take a spot. I heard a lot of people say he's going to Michigan because Stan Edwards played for Bo Schembechler, his father was heavily involved with the university, he didn't do anything for three years in high school, etc. So I had that chip early on.

Recruiting websites were just getting started, ranking high school players and giving star ratings. From when I started my senior year in high school until I got to Michigan, I knew about all of the rankings and I checked the site constantly. I was looking at rankings every day to see where I stacked up. This was before all the national camps that they have now, where the best of the best are going up against each other every week.

I looked at the websites with the pictures, stat lines, and where everyone was ranked. Because of that I knew who we had coming in and who was ranked where. I knew Marlin Jackson was a five-star and that Earnest Shazor, who went to Martin Luther King Jr. High with me, was the No. 1 ranked safety in the country and was a five-star. You had Matt Lentz, a four-star, and Pat Massey, Kelly Baraka, and Dave Underwood.

Everybody was coming in as a freshman and everyone was trying to prove themselves. Massaquoi was a four-star out of Pennsylvania, and they were high on him. He was put together, maybe a half inch taller than me at the time. I was looking at him like I have to beat this guy.

I was trying to prove that I earned being here and was going against Marlin in pads. You could tell the difference between someone who went to a really good high school and had really good coaching and matured early. It was more of a late maturation process for me, including my height. Marlin came in ready.

It was different in 7-on-7 than when we put the pads on. When you were in shirts and shorts, you're looking fast, looking good. It's kind of like going to the driving range and hitting golf balls versus actually going out on the course. Everybody looks like Davis Love III when they're on the driving range, but when you try to hit off that grass on the course, the ball isn't hitting as smooth as you want to. That's how it was once we put pads on.

With the pads on, I was getting pressed at the line of scrimmage and I had to learn how to get off the press. Not only Marlin, but also the veteran guys were a lot stronger than I. They had been working with Gittleson for two, three, or four years. It was a 21-year-old going against a 192-pound kid. I learned very early on that it was going to be more difficult in college and I couldn't get by with just speed and athleticism. I was trying to see where the edge was and where I needed to catch up. After about a week of training camp, I realized how to do things and what I needed to do. I was working a little extra on routes and catching passes. Once I started putting in that extra work, I started putting together some consistent plays and being someone who they could rely on.

Then I started seeing my reps go up. The first team was Marquise Walker and Ron Bellamy. Marquise was ridiculous. I never saw him drop a pass in training camp or spring ball; it was crazy. He was so good. Walker and Bellamy had the ones locked up, so next was Calvin Bell, and then it varied from Zia Combs to Tyrece Butler or Rudy Smith. Then the third team was Massaquoi and me or Butler and myself.

Toward the end of camp, I started getting reps with the second team and I started passing Massaquoi. At first I was just competing with Massaquoi. I said I wanted to beat this freshman out. Then it got to the point where I noticed I was ahead of him. I was getting more reps, making more plays, and knew the playbook.

I wasn't making as many mistakes now, too, which was good. When you made a mistake, Coach Campbell was going to let you know about it, the quarterback's going to let you know about it, and then Lloyd Carr was going to let you know about it. Once Coach Carr knew of a mistake, he'd say, "Goddammit, Soup, get him out of there. He doesn't want to be here." He used to say to me all the time, "Hey, 80, get over here. I'll trade your ass to Michigan State for Charles Rogers right now if you don't get it together."

It eventually became funny because he took whatever opponent was next on the schedule and would say he'd trade you for their best player at your position. But I was hearing that a lot less because I wasn't messing up. I noticed my reps were going up and I was working with the twos now. When we went with four-wide receiver sets in the two-minute packages, I was in there. That was a big deal, and it gave me a little extra confidence coming out of training camp because being in the starting four meant I would play in games. I was giving Bellamy a spell in a real two-minute drill and was one of the receivers who they needed to make a play. That was a huge deal.

Our first game in that 2001 season was against Miami of Ohio, who had Ben Roethlisberger at quarterback at the time. That was my first time running out of the tunnel as an actual Michigan Wolverine in that setting. I came out of the tunnel during my recruitment, scrimmages, and some practices, but that first time in a game was different. Now I had my helmet on, my pads on, and my No. 80 jersey with Edwards on the back. It was official. I saw the Go Blue banner. I went down the tunnel and waited for Coach Carr to say, "Let's go." I started running and heard the band start to play. I saw 112,000 people strong, cheering. I jumped, touched the banner, and started to look around and say, "Man, there's a lot of people out here." I started to think I better not drop a pass or miss an assignment.

I really noticed the crowd right after the national anthem. I had been on that sideline since I was a little kid, but I never experienced it the way I did that first time I was suited up to play. After the national anthem finished, they did the flyover, and then the place just erupted. All that stuff was incredible, but we had a game to play, too. We used to beat Miami by 30 or so, but Roethlisberger had a game that year. We still beat them 31–13, but Roethlisberger had two touchdowns, and you saw then why he would have so much success in the NFL. I played about nine plays in that game, had a couple nice blocks, which might not seem like a big deal, but it was at Michigan.

You had to be physical, and that was something I realized early on in camp. I needed to block. I needed to hit that guy under the chin and make myself known physically, and this was coming from the guy who hated hitting as a 12-year-old kid. But I was ready to hit and be physical because Coach Carr and "Soup" Campbell got more excited about a good block than a big catch. They noticed more if you blocked and sprung somebody for a nice run than if you caught a first down. They liked selfless play.

During that first game, I made sure I had a few blocks and caught my first two passes (at the end of the game in garbage time). I was living the dream at this point. I was rolling at this point, thinking everything was going well for me and this whole college thing was going to be easy.

The problem for me was that the first game happened before school actually started. So up to that point, it was just football and no classes, lectures, or tests. I learned the hard way that once school started that a thing called time management is vitally important—that and discipline. For my class schedule that first year, I had an 8:00 AM at the fish bowl, which is a big computer lab. I had a 9:00 to 11:00 at the central campus recreation building, then 11:00 to 12:00 in the same building, a lunch break from 12:00 to 1:00, a 1:00 to 1:50 class, and then team meetings started at 2:20.

With meetings started at 2:20 every day, I had to book it out of that last class as soon as it ended and catch the bus. That 36 bus dropped me right in front of Schembechler Hall. I ran inside to the locker room to get my shorts and T-shirt on and get to the meeting at 2:20. The meetings went to 3:00 or 3:15, practice started at 3:30 and went until 5:30 or 6:00, depending on what kind of mood Coach Carr was in. Then afterward, the receivers watched one-on-ones, ate at the training table, and then studied for two hours after that until 9:00 PM.

After leaving study hall, I still had to study my plays for tomorrow and on top of that I was still 18 and wanted to do

18-year-old stuff and play video games. I was 18 and not used to being on my own in a dorm room, which is kind of like a condo with no parents. It was free roam in the hallways. I was kicking it with other freshmen and was excited about being there. I was chasing females because that was natural and then I thought I was invincible and didn't need sleep.

I paid for it my freshman year because I didn't have good time management and wasn't disciplined with my schoolwork. I focused mainly on the football side, so I had bad grades that first semester. At the end of the semester, I got called into the academic advisor's office with Shari Acho and Shelly Kovacs. They called me in and said, "Braylon, your GPA is a 1.4." I was like, *I'm sorry, what?* I always had a 3.0 or higher in high school, so this was shocking to me.

I knew my parents would eventually find out anyway, so I called my mom and told her what happened, and she was in her car, driving to Ann Arbor faster than I could hang up the phone. She talked to me outside the dorms forever about what the academic side meant and how I needed to manage my time better.

After that first game, life was easy, and things were going really well for me. It was after that when I started to see some bumps along the way. The second game of the season was against Washington, and it was at Washington. This game was significant for me because it was the first road game, and we were also facing Washington's big-time freshman wide receiver, Reggie Williams. I knew that Michigan wanted Williams in my class, and there was always a rumor that the Michigan coaches waited to offer me to find out what Williams was going to do first.

Soup says that he would've taken both of us, but regardless, I knew who Williams was even back in high school. He couldn't make it to Ann Arbor for the big recruiting weekend when I visited, so he visited Michigan the week before. When I was on my trip at Michigan, he was all I heard about that whole weekend. He was a big dude, well put together. We both played the same position, so we technically weren't going to go at it against each other, but I watched his every move that game and I went in thinking I needed to beat his ass in his house. I needed to do something because this was the guy that everybody said Michigan wanted.

Long story short, I got to see why Williams was the No. 1 incoming receiver that year. He put on a show. The first catch of his college career was like a 40 yarder when he jumped over our safety, Julius Curry. I was on the sideline, like, *man I can play, but he's good.* Washington ended up beating us, and Williams had four catches for 134 yards. I saw what he looked like and what I needed to get like.

He got me that game, but I still took a lot away from it. I saw my foundation that I was building was going to be much better than his by the time we got to our senior year. I paid attention to all facets of the game. I saw the talent, but I could tell on the backside of plays he wasn't blocking. If he wasn't going to get the ball, he'd stop running. It was little stuff like that that I picked up on. He was a freak when the ball was in the air for him, but when it wasn't coming his way, that was a different story.

After that game my freshman year started to go downhill. I wouldn't find out about my grades until the first semester was over, but my freshman year was just me stubbing my toe and getting frustrated. Training camp and that first game started off so well, but it wore off very quickly.

I was seeing action nine or 10 times a game and killing it in practice. I was getting open on Todd Howard, our No. 1 cornerback. I was getting better against Jackson, who's our

No. 2 corner. I was learning the game. I wasn't doing too much homework; I was just studying football. Then I got a back injury, and it bothered me just enough. I told the coaches I was having back spasms, so I saw the trainer and got ice and heat.

I came in for treatment the next day, and they took me out of practice. Before practice somebody threw a ball, and I dove for the ball. This happened in the indoor facility, which is right in front of Coach Carr's office and his balcony on the second floor. He can see the practice field and he saw me dive for this ball when I'm supposed to be hurt, so now the coaches thought I was faking it. It was almost like my dad thinking I was faking my knee injury all over again, but this time it was with Soup and Coach Carr. So those memories of what happened with my dad built up in my head again and got me upset.

And I couldn't really talk to my dad about stuff like this because he was the type of guy who doesn't really question the establishment. He follows the rules and gets the job done no matter what. Our relationship was good at this point, though, because it transitioned from coach to almost like a veteran player, someone I could ask questions to about how I could get better and where I could improve. But when it came to something like this, Stan asked me what I was doing and to quit playing around. He was helpful in other areas and helping me stay on course on the field, but when it came to getting actual help in a frustrating situation, he wasn't the right guy for that.

This is where my mom's relationship helped because I had no outlet to go to for sympathy outside of my mom. She talked me through everything when I was dealing with that, which ultimately helped, because I got benched because they thought I was faking the injury. I didn't travel to the Penn State game and went from being in the top four to the scout team. I was demoted, and on scout team, you don't even get to wear your own jersey. You had to wear the jersey of the opponent you're playing, so that sucked.

I was starting to get depressed because everything started out so well, and it just went downhill so fast. I feel like the coaches weren't understanding me and were treating me unfairly for whatever reason and I started to think that maybe I should transfer out. Maybe this wasn't right for me, and it wasn't going to work out the way I wanted it to. I started to think that maybe I could go to Akron, who offered me in high school, or Marshall, who had Byron Leftwich. I could easily go down to Marshall and get 1,500 yards with Leftwich.

My mom talked me out of that, though, and once again told me to stay the course. She said, "Remember that your high school career didn't go on a straight path, and this won't either. Don't give up on your dream just because of one bump." I took that to heart. So I got my back healthy and went back to what got me into the top four in the first place. I was back to thinking that I belonged there and that I had to show the coaches that I could do it. I put my head down, went back to work, made sure I knew my plays, and got back into the good graces.

I earned my way back into the top four again for the Minnesota game and was getting ready to play a lot that game. I finally got a cell phone a few weeks before. My parents didn't let me have a cell phone until then, so I was excited to have my own phone. On the morning of the game, we were in the full team meeting room, and Coach Carr was in the middle of his speech, saying, "Hey, we got a team claiming to be U of M, but we're the only goddamn U of M in the Big Ten."

He was pumping us for the game we're about to play. I was sitting right in front of him, and out of nowhere, my ringtone goes off. I had this loud, annoying ringtone that sounded like a rocket going off. *PEWWWWWWW, PEWWWWWWW*. My phone was in my bag, and my bag was directly underneath me. As soon as it rang, everybody started coughing to cover it up, and I was just like a deer in headlights. I wanted to play along with everyone else and cough, but I was just frozen. I couldn't believe it happened. I eyed Coach Carr, and then the phone went off again.

He finally looked at me and asked if it's my phone. I looked down at my bag, and he kicked me out. The meetings were on the second floor, and the tradition was that when the meeting was over, we all walked down the stairwell and came out the front doors. The buses were there and the fans, family, and friends were all out in front cheering us on to get on the bus to go to the game.

I walked down by myself, opened the door, and everybody was going crazy, but it was just me. I walked out with my head down, got on the bus, and sat in the back. I didn't play one snap that game. Soup told me later on that I was going to play the whole second half of the game, but I didn't play one snap. And my phone had rang because it was my dad who called asking about tickets for the game.

It went back to me and Coach Carr not seeing eye to eye again, and I went back to scout team against Wisconsin and Ohio State. Then I found those bad grades, and Soup told me that I wouldn't be playing in the bowl game because of how poorly I did that semester. So now I was really upset. The thoughts of transferring crept up again, and I was just down on myself about everything.

Soup sat me down and said the best thing I could do was go down to bowl practices and get things right for spring ball. I went down there and tried to use it as a catapult, but I ended up spraining my ankle in a scrimmage. That was another bump in the road.

We went down to Florida. I noticed every time we went to a bowl game, Coach Carr had us going hard in practice. We had two-a-days when we played Tennessee my freshman year, we went hard my sophomore year when we played Florida, and none of these teams were practicing like we were. These guys were in shorts and T-shirts, relaxing, and all of them kicked our ass except Florida. Tennessee beat the breaks off of us, and I don't think they practiced one time.

We moved forward, though, and so did I. The season was over, and I had to treat it as if it was a new beginning to try to get back in the good graces of the coaches and get my college career back on the right track.

6

Breaking Through

DURING MY WHOLE TIME IN COLLEGE, JANUARY 2002 TO APRIL 2002 was probably the most pivotal transition for me. Winter conditioning leads into spring ball, and spring ball is where you get the jump on the next season. It's when the roster gets set for summer 7-on-7 and training camp. I was looking around, and Marquise Walker was gone. Ron Bellamy was going to be the starter, but then after him, we had Calvin Bell, Zia Combs, and Tim Massaquoi, who seemed prime for a move to tight end at that point.

The playing time was there for the taking, and on top of that, I knew we had Jason Avant, Steve Breaston, and Carl Tabb coming in this next recruiting class. They weren't there in the winter or spring, so this was my chance to get a leg up and secure my spot on the roster. I worked my tail off all winter and I was doing everything they told me to do. I was going to class. I wasn't a partier and I didn't drink, so I was just studying plays and studying school.

Then when spring ball hit, which is usually around the beginning of March, I attacked it like a savage. I was trying to knock the safeties out. I was working on moves before practice, so I could get open and beat the press. I had the best spring ball of anyone—hands down—and it wasn't even close. I put in so much work that by the end of spring ball it was Bellamy and myself as the starting two receivers.

I really knew I was doing well because I didn't hear anything from Lloyd Carr. If the head coach wasn't saying anything to you, that was a positive. It meant you were doing something right. Erik Campbell let me know how well I was doing, but Coach Carr didn't give out too much praise, so the fact that he wasn't yelling at me meant I was doing the right thing. When I asked my mom about it, she said I should just keep doing whatever it was I was doing. Soup told me, "I like what you're doing. You got to be a dog if you want to play for me and you're being a dog."

Everything was going well—even in the classroom. I got my grades up. I had a 3.7 that winter semester and got off academic probation. I carried that through to the summer and I never took summer classes so I was able to focus just on football. Everybody always asked me why I didn't take summer classes, and I told them I wanted to be able to focus on football. I said, "God doesn't have a Plan B, so why the hell should I?" I did well in school, I got a couple 4.0 semesters, but there was no doubt I was putting all my eggs in one basket.

Based on how my spring and summer went, it looked as though I had everything on track to be great. We went to training camp, and it was definitely Bellamy and me starting and then Bell as the No. 3 and Tyrece Butler as the No. 4. And then Bellamy hurt his ankle before the first game of the season, which meant I was the guy. Talk about a turn of events. I went from the scout team in December to the main guy in September. That winter and spring really set the tone for my Michigan career. The work I put in to get to that point showed me what it actually took to be great and have success.

I was upset that Bellamy hurt his ankle because Ron and I were really close, but it was interesting timing that I was now the main receiver because Reggie Williams and Washington were coming to Ann Arbor for the first game of the season. Williams was coming to my house this time. He got me the first time, so I was really eyeing him this go-around. We came out, and I had a couple catches the first drive, but I was still eyeing Williams, watching what he's doing. I was hitting their cornerback every play and was sticking the safeties. We called a play where I ran a deep post and we ran it like clockwork. John Navarre threw the ball, I jumped up, caught it, and got tackled in the end zone. It was my first collegiate touchdown, so I didn't know what to do once I caught it. I got up to celebrate, and Chris Perry knocked me over. We beat Washington and my nemesis 31–29. I got him this time, and it made me feel like I had arrived.

After the games our parents waited for us outside the tunnel outside of the stadium. I walked out this time after catching my first touchdown, and they saw me and ran right over. My mom gave me a big hug. My stepmom was second, I hugged Charles third, and then Dad always wanted to be the last one. When I would do something good, he would be like, "Okay, man, all right, I see you." That started to become a regular thing.

I had five catches for 80 yards and a touchdown that game and started to get some praise. Bellamy and I had been really close, but at that moment, I felt a little shift in our relationship. He was hurt and saw that I was starting to ball. The next week I had two touchdowns against Western Michigan, so I had three touchdowns through two weeks of the season.

I didn't realize it at the time, but that shift came with Bellamy because it was his turn. He played his freshman year and scored three touchdowns his freshman year. He had to play behind David Terrell that year and then Walker the next year. It was his junior year and it was supposed to be his year, and here came me, another guy he had to deal with. Once he came back from his injury, that tension went away, and we were back to normal again. He came back and caught up right where he left off, so there was no anxiety about missing out or losing his spot anymore.

But I was still rising. In the fourth game of the season against Utah, I had my first 100-yard game and had my first postgame TV interview with Holly Rowe and ESPN. Our communications guy, Dave Ablauf, told me ESPN wanted to talk to me, and I couldn't believe it. *They want to talk to me? I'm going to be on TV?* When I got into the locker room after the interview, all my classmates started yelling, "Uh oh, new money in the building."

Things started to change on campus, too. Even though we played ball, we were still out there in class like regular students. I started to hear, "Hey, Braylon, you're out there killing it." We're going to frat parties, and the groupies started to come around, saying, "Oh my gosh, it's Braylon Edwards." Before this I was riding the bus through campus with no one recognizing me or asking for an autograph. Nobody knew who I was before, and then I was being asked to sign their dorm room door. It was stuff I saw in movies and now it's starting to happen to me.

When that happens to a kid, a 19-year-old kid who has always tried to fit in and always tried to find his place, it's only natural that it starts to go to your head. It impacted me, and I ended up letting go of certain things. I was physical when I wanted to be but not all the time. I ran hard but not all the time. I was still clowning around a little bit, too, which I knew the coaches didn't like. We played Penn State, and at the time Penn State was 4–1. They were good. They had Larry Johnson, Michael Haynes, Anthony Adams, and Robbie Gould. They were rolling when they were coming to play us.

The night before a home game, it was always movie night at the Campus Inn, where we stayed. We had to keep the latch open

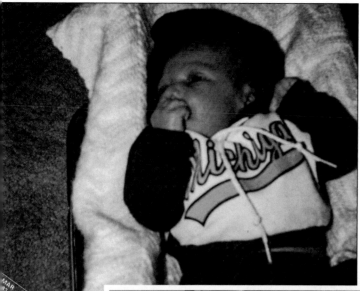

From just about birth,
I was a Michigan fan.
(*Malesa Plater*)

My mom,
Malesa Plater,
holds me when
I am only days old.
(*Malesa Plater*)

I won the CYO in track
during my eighth-grade
year at U of D.
(*Malesa Plater*)

I pose on the track, where I began running competitively at age nine. *(Malesa Plater)*

Not only was I good at track, I initially liked it more than football. *(Malesa Plater)*

After football season I ran track at the University of Michigan. An added bonus was that it got me out of winter conditioning with the football team, which was brutal. *(Malesa Plater)*

My father, Stan Edwards, a track coach and former NFL player, was instrumental in helping me become a professional athlete. *(Malesa Plater)*

take great pride in that No. 1 jersey, and my stepfather, Charles, is always proud of my accomplishments. *(Malesa Plater)*

From left to right: my cheering section (my mom, Malesa Plater; my stepmom, Carolyn; and my sister, Jade) attended almost every one of my college games. *(Malesa Plater)*

We lost a physical contest at Oregon in 2003. I struggled with drops because of torn ligaments in my finger but still had 144 receiving yards.

I celebrate my 40-yard touchdown reception during our 2003 road victory at Michigan State.

I celebrate the 35–21 win against Ohio State, a victory that clinched the Big Ten title and sent us to the Rose Bowl, with The Big House crowd in 2003.

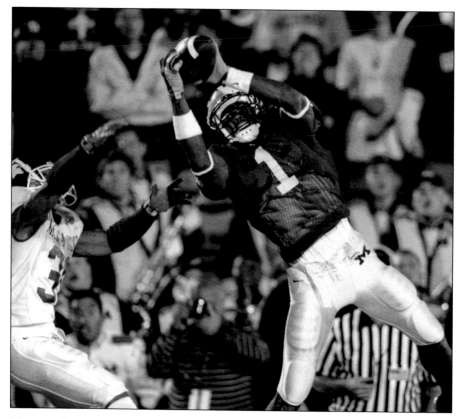

My 22-yard touchdown catch against Michigan State sends the 2004 game, an epic grudge match we won 45–37, into overtime.

I haul in one of my 11 catches, which went for a total of 172 receiving yards, in my final game against Ohio State. (Getty Images)

During a heartbreaking 38–37 loss to Texas, I haul in one of my three touchdown passes in the Rose Bowl.

I remain close with my former Michigan receiver coach, Erik "Soup" Campbell.

From left to right: Erik Campbell, my college position coach; Charles, my stepdad; me; and Stan Edwards, my dad; pose in 2005. *(Malesa Plater)*

From left to right: Stan Edwards, my dad; Malesa Plater, my mom; me; Carolyn, my stepmom; and Charles, my stepdad; are part of my B team, as I coined them during my pro career. *(Malesa Plater)*

on our doors in our rooms, so the trainers could leave snacks in the room and the coaches could do bed check. So guys snuck upstairs during the movie and pulled pranks. Chris went up to my room and turned my thermostat all the way up. That used to be the running joke. I got in my room, and it was 90 degrees in there. I knew it was Chris because we went back and forth at each other, and his room was right next to mine, so I was going to get him back. I heard him shut his door and through my peephole I saw him walk down the hall. He walked out the exit door to the stairs to go meet his girlfriend in the lobby.

When he went out the door, I went in his room and took all of his pillows and covers. While I was in the process of doing that, he came back up from the stairs and saw me. He grabbed one of his pillows from my hands, I threw the covers in my room, and we started pillow fighting in the hallway. We're really going at it and then we dropped the pillows. We were about to go to blows because he hit me really hard. I couldn't see out of my left eye, so I was upset. Coach Carr's room happened to be right next to Chris' room. Coach Carr came out in his T-shirt and jogging pants and said, "Hey, Goddammit. Take your sons of bitches, get back in your room."

We played Penn State the next day, and Chris and I were benched for the first half because of the pillow fight. With about six minutes left in the game, we're down 14. Chris and I had been looking at each other the whole game like we couldn't lose this game after last night. Chris was a junior, so he already had a relationship with Coach Carr. I was a sophomore, so I was still trying to find my relationship like that. I was like, *if we lose this game, especially after last night, I'm going to Toledo because I'm definitely getting kicked out.*

I scored a touchdown with about 13 minutes left and then I scored another one with about three minutes left to tie it up. After I helped get us back in the game after Coach Carr got so mad at us, that was a huge relief. We went into overtime, and Penn State kicked a field goal. We got the ball, and Chris scored a touchdown to win the game. Chris and I were so relieved. It was no coincidence that he and I scored the last three touchdowns in that game. It had to happen that way, and we made sure that we did what we needed to do. Coach Carr still made us go to the stadium every day at 5:00 AM for two weeks because of that pillow fight. He told me, "You're lucky. You would've been wearing blue and gold, but it wouldn't have been here."

That kind of thing happened every now and then, and Coach Carr never liked me clowning around. On top of that, I got a little lippy with Soup and Coach Carr sometimes, too. We were about to play Minnesota, and I ran a route in practice where I caught a pass. When you made a catch in practice, the coaches wanted you to turn and run an extra 10 yards after you caught it and then run back to the huddle. I caught the pass and I was tired, so I started walking back to the huddle. Coach Carr looked at me and told me to run, so I looked at him and said I was tired. He said, "You're what? Get your ass out of practice." Soup walked with me and asked me what was wrong, and I said I was tired.

I was feeling myself and poking my chest out a little bit because people were calling my name. At this point I was battling with Charles Rogers, Michael Jenkins, and John Standeford for All-Big Ten honors, so I was feeling good and started to act a different way. I got benched for the Minnesota game because of that; I didn't play the first two series. I was pouting on the sideline, and Soup told me to quit pouting and be ready to go.

Soup put me in the game after we were losing to Minnesota. I caught a touchdown on a fade route and then I caught a deep over that set up a Perry touchdown. Then I caught a deep bomb. I didn't say anything to Soup or Coach Carr after the game, but Coach Carr saw me the next day in the hallway and said, "Am I going to have a problem with you this week? I don't know what you have going on in your mind, but you played damn well in that second half... That's the guy I want to see."

I looked right at him and told him, "That's the guy I've been. I've been that guy."

He said, "You just don't get it." Then he made me wake up at 5:00 AM that whole week because I mouthed off to him. I felt like I shouldn't be there again. I felt like Soup didn't really have my back either. Your position coach was supposed to keep you in line but also be a buffer between you and the head coach, and I wasn't getting that from Soup at this point.

I woke up at 5:00 AM that whole week. When we played Illinois, I had four catches, 101 yards, and another touchdown. I got to the point then where I just wasn't going to say anything to anyone when it was time for business. I was normally the class clown, cracking jokes on people and imitating some of the other players and coaches, but I just got in this mode where I thought everything I did and said got me in trouble, so I was just going to keep my head down and my mouth shut. I went into this zone where I just wasn't talking to the coaches and even some of my teammates at Schembechler Hall.

I talked to my teammates outside of Schembechler, but I stayed disciplined and in my zone the rest of my sophomore year, which got me through that season. I didn't want to keep on this roller coaster, where I would take two steps forward and then one step back with Coach Carr. I knew some of it was self-inflicted, but I also felt like a lot of it was them being hard on me because I was Stan's kid and I could handle it.

A part of me even thought that it was because I was a three-star in high school. Would they have done that to Navarre if his cell phone went off? I don't know, but it was frustrating to deal with because I just kept stubbing my toe and going backward when all I wanted to do was go forward. My goal that year was to get first-team All-Big Ten, but I didn't do it. I finished second team and watched Rogers get first-team honors. The competitor in me was upset, and I knew that things needed to change for me if I was really going to be one of the best receivers in the conference.

7

The Rose Bowl and a Big Decision

THE FURTHER I GOT INTO MY COLLEGE CAREER, THE MORE I started to really size myself up against other receivers and see how we compared. My freshman season it was Reggie Williams, and at the end of my junior season, my new nemesis became Mike Williams. Mike was a big receiver at USC and was one of the guys everyone was talking about. He had the opportunity to play with Carson Palmer and then Matt Leinart at quarterback. Mike was being called the No. 1 receiver in college football, and I thought that was bullshit. He was going to have to prove that. He had the chance to prove it my junior season when we played USC in the Rose Bowl.

The whole time we're preparing to play USC, I'm preparing to play against him. It was the same thing as when we played Reggie's Washington Huskies in that we didn't even play against each other since we played the same position, but I wanted to have a better game than him and show everyone who the better receiver was. At this point I was also starting to think about the other side. I had put up some really good numbers my junior season, and the NFL would be an option. That line of thought really started after the Minnesota game where I had almost 100 yards receiving and a touchdown. From the Ohio State game to January 1, I was training as if that could be an option and that it was my last season at Michigan.

I was training like it's a fight once again, as if Charles was humming the *Rocky* theme music. I heard that in my head and I was just ready to go to battle and beat this so-called No. 1 receiver. I wanted to beat him and the whole team because it was a juggernaut. They had Mike, Leinart, Reggie Bush, Mike Patterson, Darnell Bing, and Shaun Cody. The whole team was ridiculous, but we could beat them.

We got the ball first in the game, and I was ready to destroy Mike. It was third and 4 on the first series, and the coaches called a go route. I blew by Will Poole, but I never knew the sun was that bright on the West Coast. I got by Poole, looked up, and the ball hit my facemask and gloves and went out of bounds. I was sick. That play cost me the rest of the game because I was just out of it mentally. I still had 10 catches for 107 yards, but that was a precursor for how this game would go for us. The way that ball hit my facemask should've told us to prepare for what was going to happen. John Navarre threw a ball on a slant and he threw it so bad that it hit my cleat, bounced up, and was caught by Lofa Tatupu. How does that happen?

Mike had this ridiculous play against Leon Hall on a comeback route. He slapped Hall so hard at the line of scrimmage that Hall actually fell down. Mike should've just run a go route because it was so wide open. He almost caused an interception because he slapped Hall so hard that Hall fell in the throwing lane of the comeback route. But Mike just jumped over Hall to grab the ball, and I had to admit this guy was good.

We end up losing that game 28–14, and now I seriously started thinking about whether I should stay at Michigan or go to the NFL. *Do I go and make millions and fulfill my lifelong dream?* I started to ask myself and the people around me all kinds of questions to help make the decision. *Is my Michigan experience over?*

Am I the best wide receiver I can be? Did I do all I could do and leave the right legacy?

It was a decision process that my family and I wanted to make together. Both sets of parents were involved with everyone's input on what we should do. They were there when it all started, and I wanted them to be there if this was the end. We wanted to do everything right, so we looked at agents and found somebody that we liked, but we wanted to go and talk to Lloyd Carr first and see what he thought.

We set up a meeting with Coach Carr, and I think what my dad and I were trying to get out of the meeting was for Coach Carr to tell us that Michigan needed me and that I should come back to school to help the team, that Michigan couldn't do it without me, and that they'd give me the keys to the offense. That's what I wanted to hear, but it's not what we got. What we got was: "Well, you have to do what's best for you. If you think you should leave, then leave. If you think you should stay, then stay. You've been fun to be around, but nothing lasts forever."

It was the most dry conversation I've ever had, and then I was thinking there's like no appreciation here. After that meeting I wanted to leave because it felt as though Coach Carr was saying it didn't matter if I was there or not. I didn't need him to beg me to come back, but I wanted to know that I mattered and he appreciated what I did. On top of that, I had dealt with getting punished, getting the No. 1 jersey taken away, them thinking I faked injuries. I couldn't go through all of that again my senior year.

After we walked out of that meeting, I looked at my dad, my mom, and stepdad and I thought I was leaving. We put my name in to get a draft grade and see where my potential draft slot would be for that year. We got the report back, and it said the highest they saw for me was No. 10 overall, and that was based on what I did in college and if I had a monster combine and pro day. The lowest they saw was the middle of the second round. That was a big discrepancy, and I didn't know if I wanted to risk millions if it went to the latter half of that projection.

I sat and thought on it and decided I should ask my grandma what she thought. This was the church lady who I never crossed when I was younger. There's no better person to give it to you straight than your grandma, so I sought her out to see if she had any wisdom to lend me. I told her I was conflicted and didn't know what to do. She first told me to pray on it, of course, but then she asked me if I was done at Michigan. She asked if I accomplished everything I sought out to do, and if I left Michigan now, would I eventually be upset that I left?

These questions started to really make me think. I was only thinking about if I would get drafted top 10 or not. I began to think about what I had done at Michigan. I was second-team All-Big Ten my sophomore year, first-team All-Big Ten my junior year, and honorable mention All-American my junior year. I didn't win the Fred Biletnikoff Award for the top receiver. We did win a Big Ten championship, but I didn't graduate.

The more and more I thought about who I was rather than where I would be drafted, it became clear to me. I felt like I wasn't the most polished receiver I could be, that there were weak parts in my game. Then I thought about that discrepancy between being the No. 10 overall pick and a mid-second round pick, and there's a big difference there. I thought then that it might be right for me to come back, but I sought out a few more people just to make sure.

At the same time, I was trying to make my decision, Marlin Jackson and Dave Baas also had the opportunity to leave. All three of us were heading into our final year, so we got together and talked about what each of us was thinking and if we all wanted to come back together and make this final season the best one yet. Jackson was a freshman All-American who balled out his sophomore year, but they switched him to safety his junior season. He had on okay year, but he got banged up so he didn't have the year he wanted either. I said for me it was too big of a difference being picked 10 or 48. Plus, I didn't like the way we lost to USC, Iowa, and Oregon that season. The other thing for me was the quarterback situation. I knew Navarre was leaving, but I trusted Matt Gutierrez.

We all thought about it and decided we wanted our M rings and thought we could reach a national championship game. I said I was coming back. Marlin said he needed to come back, and then Bass looked at us and said, "Those who stay." The linemen are always the corny ones, but I said I would let him have that one because he was right. The Michigan mantra is: "those who stay will be champions." And we wanted to be champions. All three of us were coming back.

But we weren't just coming back and hoping it would get better. If we were going to sacrifice potentially millions of dollars in the NFL, then we were going to do it right. We're coming back with a whole different mind-set. We knew we were going to be the three who would get the team going and be leaders of the team. We had other seniors that would help, too, but everyone had to fall in line. We didn't want any excuses or bullshit. We're going to go after it.

If you had to stop partying so much, then do it. I didn't drink until I turned 21, so I was drinking by this time, but all of that was secondary now. We were focused and determined that spring ball through summer and training camp would be the best we've ever had. We were policing ourselves now because we wanted everything right. We told the coaches that if anything happened to let us deal with it in-house, and the coaches gave us the right to do so.

We used to run on the golf course right next to the stadium in Ann Arbor, and I didn't like running distances, and the golf course run certainly qualified. My sophomore year I got into it with Mike Gittleson because I always finished close to last when we ran the golf course. He always asked me how I finished last if I'm one of the fastest guys on the team, and I said it was because I was fast but didn't have or want the endurance to run almost four miles. I asked him, "When I am ever going to run 3.7 miles on the football field?" Teams like Miami were running 100 repeats, 40 shuttles, gassers with the parachutes behind them. That stuff was getting them explosive, and we're running 3.7 miles and we're Michigan Men because we finished.

My senior year, though, I always finished in the top 10 in the golf course run. I improved my bench up from doing 25 reps of 225 pounds to 33, and everything just started to change for us. We told Adam Stenavich, Matt Lentz, and Tyler Eckert the plan and said, "Let's crush it." We told the scout team to give us a good look every week. Sometimes in practice with the scout team, you told them to chill out a little bit, that we're tired, so relax. This year we weren't doing that. It was 100 percent every play so we were ready.

We did bag drills where the coaches would lay out these long blue bags that you ran over and side to side while avoiding the bags. They laid out seven bags, and Gittleson yelled out numbers that were divisible by seven. If he yelled out 77, that meant we needed to run 11 times back and forth or 77 times. Guys were dying, getting sloppy, knocking bags over. But this year we addressed it and said we had to be ready to attack those bags. It got to the point where he was yelling 154, which would have been 22 times, and we weren't blinking.

We all started to see that work pay off, too, even in the summer. Some of my high school friends went to MAC schools, and some went to Michigan State, which was basically like a MAC school then. We did 7-on-7 stuff in the summer and we all met up at 13 Mile Road and Lahser to get work in. I was on such a different level at this point when we did one-on-ones. I looked at them like kids. I was a first-team All-Big Ten guy who just benched 225 pounds 33 times and I went against two first-round corners in practice in Marlin and Leon, so this was nothing. I was no longer the Martin Luther King Jr. or Bishop Gallagher High kid trying to find myself. I was through the roof, and that neighborhood stuff was over.

Greg Harden also was really pivotal in getting me to this point mentally, where I was focused on my future and no longer clowning around. Greg has helped a ton of athletes with the mental health side of the equation. He played a big role with both Tom Brady and Desmond Howard while they were in Ann Arbor. Harden was basically a life coach and a motivational speaker who helped you get through whatever it was you're dealing with mentally.

My mom, dad, and stepdad were always there in different facets of my life, but Greg was able to make me think a certain way and get me to really wrap your head around an issue. Whether I was depressed, thinking about transferring, or dealing with success or disappointment, he was there for me. Throughout all the transitional phases of my time in Ann Arbor, Harden was there to help me through everything. He did it in a way where he would let me figure it out, too. He didn't just tell me the solution.

He guided me to the solution and allowed me to think my way through it. He said, "Braylon, he took the No. 1 jersey and gave 80 back to you. How does that make you feel?" But then he'd say, "How can you get it back? You were angry, but you have a part in this, too. So how do you fix it?"

Even if you hadn't done anything wrong and you were right in the situation, he helped you figure out a way to get the other person to see your side. We talked so much up to this year that it got to the point where I didn't even make appointments. I just had walk-ins. I knocked on the door and said, "Hey, G. It's your favorite." Harden put me on the path to enlightenment, and allowing me to figure out the conflict myself made it so much more meaningful in the long run.

When I started to know how to use his exercises and figure things out on my own, I didn't need to rely on him so much. I saw him a lot my sophomore and junior year and then my senior year I saw him maybe twice in his office. He was a therapist before it was okay for athletes to see a therapist and he was a huge reason why I made it through college the way I did.

Greg was a factor in why I came back that senior year, too, because I knew I had a lot of resources available to me. Another reason was that Erik Campbell and I had become really close. I had earned his trust through hard work my junior season. There was no more snitching on me when I was late to a practice mainly because I was never late, but it got to the point where he never had to correct me in practice or a game. We weren't equals, but we could kick it as friends, and he didn't have to hold my hand anymore. I became a player/coach for him where he could tell the young guys to watch how I ran or executed a drill in practice, which was invaluable to him. I was there a few hours early before practice watching film. I was trying to put guys in the ground in blocking drills, and there was no more arguing or mouthing off to Soup either.

A lot of the negative aspects I had dealt with before and the roadblocks that were in front of me had been cleared for my senior season. But we still had the season ahead of us and had to put it all together on the field because we had some bad losses in the last few years. Our freshman year we got cheated by Michigan State. That was the infamous stop-the-clock game. Because of Michigan State they implemented the rule where they keep the time on the field now and not in the press box. That year we get to one of the final plays and we were all thinking we were going to beat the Spartans because time was about to expire. We stopped quarterback Jeff Smoker two yards shy of the end zone, and he tried to spike the ball. That should've ended the game, but they gave him one second, which lasted an eternity, and he threw a pass to T.J. Duckett to give Michigan State the 26–24 win. Larry Foote threw his helmet at the officials, and Coach Carr said we deserved better.

The Spartans cheated us, and we would've beaten them that year. But we all started asking ourselves: *how do we make it so we're not a play away? How do we make that play? How do we not play down to a team that's not as good as us?* The answer was that we needed to hold people accountable and make sure the freshmen were coming in with the right mentality. When 18-year-olds come in, they're playful and think things are funny; I know, I was in the same boat. They were not necessarily going to start or play, so they didn't treat each practice the way we did.

We were on those freshmen and made them lead a lot of the runs, some of the drills, and held them accountable as if it was their last year, too. We had Mike Hart, Morgan Trent, and Alan Branch, who we used to call Uncle Phil because he looked like

Uncle Phil from the show, *The Fresh Prince of Bel-Air*. We had Chad Henne, a five-star quarterback out of Pennsylvania, and we had Henne lead a lot of the drills, even though Gutierrez was still there.

The seniors all made sure we spent time with the younger guys and Hart, Trent, and Adrian Arrington eventually were like my little brothers. We built that bond. I think the toughest thing for the young players to see is the concept of playing for your brother. They get it when you play Ohio State because that's the last game. But we wanted them to have that attitude all year long.

Part of what made us confident that we would be able to get everyone to buy into this mentality was because we had a solid quarterback situation. Henne was there as a freshman, but we were all confident in what Gutierrez could do. Truthfully, Gutierrez was part of the reason why I came back for that final season because I trusted him and liked what he had done up to this point. He was a year younger than I, so I saw what he was doing in practice and was comfortable with what he was doing the year prior. We hung out a lot, too. Gutierrez was white, but he's a brother. He was dating the friend of the girl I was dating, and we just had our own chemistry. In spring ball that year, we lit it up. Gutierrez would just give me this look, and I would know he was coming to me with the ball. Summer went well, 7-on-7 went well, and then we got to training camp. We had Gutierrez and one of the best wide receiver corps in the country.

We had Steve Breaston, an eccentric cat who's writing poetry and writing raps. He was a Mos Def/woke character. We had Jason Avant, who is a born-again Baptist. He didn't listen to rap music, and you couldn't curse around him; everything was spiritual. And then you had me, the class clown. We're three different people, but Gutierrez had a relationship with each one of us.

We got to training camp, and all of the sudden, Gutierrez didn't look the same as he did from spring ball to summer. We're trying to figure it out and we thought maybe he was scared of Henne. They made a lot of noise about Henne, so maybe he's folding under the pressure. We got to the third week, and his throws weren't where they should be. He's struggling on the deep ball and throwing a lot of interceptions. Gutierrez started getting down on himself, and I didn't want to make it a me thing, but we needed him to be successful.

After camp finished and on the Saturday before the first game of the season against Miami of Ohio, Soup called me and said, "I just wanted to tell you Chad's going to start this week. Don't tell nobody." I was like, *a freshman?* I asked what happened to Gutierrez, and Soup said he tore his labrum the week before. They had run X-rays, but back then if everything looked good on X-ray, then you were fine. They finally did an MRI, and it showed a separation of his labrum, which is why his throws were off.

This was my high school career happening all over again. At Bishop Gallagher when I thought I was in a good place at quarterback, an injury happened, and we had to start a freshman. The only positive out of it happening now was that I had already been through it before at Gallagher, and I knew how to handle it this time around. Plus, Henne wasn't coming in with a young, inexperienced offense. He had an unbelievable wide receiver corps and Lentz, Stenavich, and Baas on the offensive line. He had a lot of senior leadership in that huddle to help him. Plus, he was prepared because we had forced him to lead the team in training camp. We were lucky that we did that because then Henne was already prepared to lead and to take over the team.

We were all nervous, though, because it's still a freshman. Henne was a five-star guy, and everyone wanted him, but he's

still a freshman, and we're trying to win a national championship. I found out very early in that season, though, that Henne
was ahead of most young quarterbacks. In that first game
against Miami of Ohio, we had a play called Spartan, which had
two deep over routes, and then we had a Spartan Z out, where
instead of two overs you had to run an out route off of an underneath route.

The first time we ran it, I was wide open. If he hit me in stride,
I would've walked in for a 60-yard touchdown. But he threw it
behind me, so I had to jump back and catch it. I fell down as
a result because my momentum shifted. We ran the same play
in the second quarter, and he threw it right in stride. I caught it,
jumped over the safety, and scored. I thought, *wow, he learned
from his mistakes very quickly.* He threw these short mesh routes,
which are maybe six yards from the offensive tackle, and threw
it so hard. He had a cannon, and one of them bounced off my
hands and off my chest, but I still caught it. I went back to the
huddle and told him to ease up. So he came out in the second
half and put some touch on it. I saw his ability to adapt in game
from that first game, which was promising.

We had some hope at quarterback, but the only problem now
was that we didn't have a running back. Hart wasn't playing yet,
so the coaches were cycling through the running backs to figure
out who would be the guy, and no one was really doing much
of anything. We went to Notre Dame and got beat because we
didn't have a run game and because the coaches closed the playbook for Henne. They didn't let him open it up, and here we
went again, losing another game we shouldn't lose.

The coaches went back to the drawing board, and that's when
Mike started playing against San Diego State. That is when the
season started to take off for us because the coaches let Henne

and Mike play their game. The first play of the game against San Diego State, we ran a double move go route, and it was a touchdown to me up the right sideline. We come back with another go route to start the second half. I dove and caught it, but that wasn't the story of the game. The story was Mike Hart.

I have never seen anyone besides Barry Sanders who can make the first two guys miss like Mike could. I don't care how bad the protection was. Nobody was touching him. He knew how to hit the creases. He wasn't fast, but he could shake, so we called him "Little Scoot Scoot." He made plays, and we were all excited because now we had something and knew we could make some noise despite that Notre Dame loss.

As the season progressed, I started stacking myself against the other receivers across the country again. It was Mark Clayton from Oklahoma and myself. Mike Williams tried to leave school that previous year when Maurice Clarett challenged the NFL's rule that required a player to wait three years before gaining eligibility to the NFL draft. The judge initially ruled that Clarett could leave, so Williams hired an agent and declared as well. That ruling was reversed, though, and Williams wasn't allowed back at school, so he wasn't in the conversation anymore.

Looking back at my decision to stay in school, I was happy I did. There were seven receivers drafted in the first round of that draft my junior year: Roy Williams, Larry Fitzgerald, Reggie Williams, Lee Evans, Michael Clayton, Rashaun Woods, and Michael Jenkins. Fitzgerald and Roy Williams would have gone before me, and I'm pretty sure Reggie Williams would have gone before me, too, so I would've been the fourth receiver taken in that draft. That would've put me around 13 to the Buffalo Bills, and that's a big difference from where I was actually drafted.

I was happy I stayed. Making me even happier was that we now had a quarterback, a running back, and a great all-around offense. My stats kept rising, and I was putting together a great season. We destroyed Iowa, we beat Indiana, and then that great season started to hit some road bumps.

We played Minnesota at home and we beat them bad my freshman year, but my sophomore year they almost beat us. This time we only won by three, and people acted like that Minnesota game didn't even happen. We just struggled on offense, the passing game wasn't working, and then I was in a funk. We're over the halfway point, and my numbers started to take a dip. Against San Diego State, Iowa, and Indiana, I had 22 receptions for 445 yards and five touchdowns. Against Minnesota, Illinois, and Purdue, I had 18 receptions for 141 yards and one touchdown.

This wasn't the way we wanted to enter the Michigan State game, which was next on the schedule. This was supposed to be a national championship-type season, and even though we had one loss, we still had a lot on the line. If we were going to do anything big that season, we needed to get through Michigan State. It was already working up to be a big game in my mind, but I had no idea how incredible it would actually be.

8

The Michigan State
Comeback

DURING THE SECOND GAME OF THE 2004 SEASON, WE LOST TO Notre Dame, but after that loss, we put together a string of six wins before the Michigan State game. We were ranked No. 11 and were still undefeated in conference play, so there was a lot left on the table for us. Though we were just outside the top 10, Michigan State wasn't ranked and had a 4–3 record. It wasn't a bad team, even though the record indicated it was. Plus, we couldn't get the passing game going and were in a little bit of a funk ourselves. So we knew it wasn't going to be an easy game.

We looked pretty good on the opening drive of the game. Mike Hart had some runs and scored a touchdown. But after that it became the Drew Stanton and DeAndra Cobb show. Stanton was doing anything he wanted. Cobb had two touchdowns, Michigan State was running all over us, and this game is what started the collapse of our defense.

Michigan State was having its way with us, and it wasn't looking good. Then, right before the half, LaMarr Woodley clobbered Stanton and drove him into the ground. Stanton landed on his throwing shoulder and separated it. I do not condone celebrating injuries, but when that happened, everyone on our sideline gave a collective sigh of relief, and it was in unison. Stanton had the Spartans going on all cylinders, so we thought maybe if he's out of the game, things would slow down.

We headed into halftime down 17–10, which doesn't sound all that bad on paper, but Michigan State was building momentum and had everything on its side. We were in the locker room, saying we needed to figure this out. Lloyd Carr tried to light a fire under our butt by yelling at us. Coach Carr's biggest thing was to never get pushed around in your own home; he was firm on that. We were getting pushed around in our home, and it was Michigan State doing the pushing.

Coach Carr told us to have some pride in ourselves and that this wasn't Michigan football. He looked at the seniors and asked us if we wanted to lose our last game against Michigan State and if that was how we wanted to go out this season. I don't know about the rest of the seniors, but that clicked for me. I thought back to the conversations I had with Marlin Jackson and David Baas about changing the mind-set and changing the way the season went our last time around.

We didn't want to give games away to teams like we did in the past and here we were doing it again. We needed to win this game. I thought, *if we lose this game to Michigan State, I can never say I beat them my last time. That's not happening.*

We're all fired up, and Coach Carr got us in the right mind-set, but we came out of halftime, and it was much of the same. Every time I looked up, it's another Cobb touchdown. Damon Dowdell replaced Stanton at quarterback and he was still doing what the offense needed him to do. He was moving the ball and making plays.

We were down 17 in the fourth quarter. Then I got into make-it-happen mode, where I wanted to take over the game. The first possession of the second half, Chad Henne threw me an out route on second down, and I was thinking this was going to be the play where we get some momentum. As I was fighting for yards, trying to make something happen, I fumbled the ball. Eric Smith recovered the fumble right before he went out of bounds. I swear he went out of bounds, but Michigan State got the ball back.

The Spartans ended up kicking a field goal and were up 20–10 in the fourth quarter. They got the ball back again after a bad drive by us and they scored a touchdown. Cobb went crazy and ran for 64 yards, just like he was doing the rest of the night. That put them up 27–10 with a little more than eight minutes left in the fourth quarter.

When we were about to take the field on the ensuing drive, I looked up at my dad, who was about five rows behind our bench in the stands, and he was swiping his chest vertically. He's making the No. 1 on his chest. He was telling me it was my time. It was like, *you asked for that number and you know what came with this number. You know what time it is.*

After a couple of nice plays, we called a go route from about the 35. I said, "Okay, this is it. This play is going to kick the momentum in." If we wanted to win this game, this play had to be made. It's one-on-one coverage, and I'd been begging for the ball all day. Henne dropped back and threw the ball. I had the corner beat, but the ball was a little underthrown. I stepped back behind Roger Maples, who I played against in high school, caught the ball and fell. When I stepped back and caught it, he fell, too. Had I not fallen down I would've scored; there was nobody in front of me.

We got a field goal to put us down 14 points with a little more than six minutes to go in the game. As bad as we'd played, it's only 14 points. None of us were hanging our heads or thinking we were out of this game because it was only two touchdowns. It was 27–13, and Coach Carr felt like we needed to kick an onside kick. They never work, so I was nervous about it. We needed to get this onside kick if we're going to have a shot at winning this game; otherwise we're just giving them the ball back with good field position.

I was on the field for the onside kick. It was like it happened in slow motion. Garrett Rivas kicked it, and I was the guy who was supposed to try to catch the ball before it went out of bounds on the sideline. I saw a Michigan State player commit the one sin you cannot make on an onside kick. You never attack the ball; you let it come to you, and if it comes in your space, then you corral it. That dude ran up to secure it, and it bounced off his basket. I just yelled, "get it!" I saw Brian Thompson jump on it and I knew the game was over once we recovered it.

If we got that onside kick, I just knew we were going to win that game. Everything was starting to line up for us, so I just knew we were going to be good. We got the ball at the 38-yard line, and Michigan State had this corner on me, who was their leading rusher the year before. This little dude named Jaren Hayes had more than 600 yards rushing in 2003, and then Michigan State had him on me with the game on the line. It was almost disrespectful. I was the No. 1 receiver in the country.

I went into that drive with that mentality, that they were disrespecting me by putting a running back on me. They weren't going to stop me the rest of the game. Before we got on the field, we huddled up on the sideline. Scot Loeffler was on the headphones about to relay the play in to Erik Campbell, who took the play onto the field during sideline huddles. Then Coach Carr got in the huddle and yelled, "Goddammit, throw it up to Braylon." On the first play, we ran a sweep with Hart so we had more space to the right side because Henne liked to throw it to the right. The very next play was a go route. I got the play call and thought, *Dad said here it is. So go prove why you're the No. 1.*

Henne stepped back and threw the ball up. I was behind the cornerback, and the ball was a little short. The corner had it because I'm behind him. In that split second, I told myself: *there's no way in hell it can go down like this. If he intercepts this, it's nobody's fault but mine.* I jumped up and grabbed the ball away from him for the touchdown. That got me going. I caught it, and the crowd went crazy. I pumped my arms down toward the ground, and my teammates were screaming. We're down 27–20 with 6:12 left in the game.

If we scored one touchdown in 15 seconds, we can score another in six minutes. I was ready to go. Michigan State ran the clock down to a little more than three minutes with its drive but didn't score. The defense got us a stop and got us the ball back, and I just thought it was inevitable that we would score again. It had to work out that way.

We got the ball and we did the same thing to them again. Hart ran the ball, came back to the line of scrimmage, and I saw Coach yelling from the sideline to throw it up to me. Henne threw it up—a beautiful throw—and I set up the defensive back by being behind him. He didn't really see me. So he didn't put his body on me. He thought he had the ball, and I just jumped between the ball and him and went and got it. We tied the game at 27 with three minutes left in the game.

If you watch the replay of that catch, you can see the fans going crazy and just losing it, but if you look at me in the pictures or videos, you'll see I'm in a zone. I just didn't lose my focus after that catch like I did the one prior to that. The band director was going nuts behind me, but I knew it wasn't over. I was dialed in and thinking about overtime. I wasn't thinking about how we came back or that I caught the game-tying touchdown. I was thinking that we need to get to overtime to secure the win.

A lot happened in that last three minutes, though. Michigan State got the ball and then punted, we got the ball and punted, and then the Spartans finally get into field-goal range with a few seconds left in regulation. They had a kicker named Dave Rayner, who played in the same high school All-Star Game that I did. We played on the East team, and the West team actually had a kicker who got a scholarship to Michigan State while Rayner walked on.

Rayner had a leg, though. He had a kick from about 52 yards, and everybody on the sideline was getting ready for overtime. I knew Rayner's leg from our time together, so I was thinking that he could make this thing. However, I still thought we were going to win the game because there were too many positive things going for us. Fortunately, he missed the field goal, and we went to overtime.

We didn't get anything going on offense in overtime, and the defense was double covering me now. We ended up kicking a field goal, and Michigan State came down and made a field goal to send it to the second overtime. After that it was just destined for us to win the game. We weren't the main game that day on television, but we were on ABC, and the game was obviously running long. All the other 3:30 games were finished at this time, so everyone was watching us.

In the second overtime, Michigan State scored quickly. We got the ball, and I caught a pass for a first down and got a few extra yards. On third down we threw a pass to Jason Avant. I may have had three touchdowns in this game, but Avant had the best catch of that game. Henne threw him open and to the back of the end zone. Avant laid out for it and somehow got his foot in bounds in the back of the end zone to send it to triple overtime.

Then we went to the third overtime, where you have to go for a two-point conversion if you score. Hart got a few yards on first down but nowhere on second down. We had the ball first, so we were thinking that we can't give them the ball after scoring another field goal. That wasn't going to work. At that point in the game, we weren't necessarily tired, but we certainly were mentally drained. But Soup always taught me to hone in on your technique when you're tired late in the game. That will always carry you. All that practice and hard work was going to pay off on this third-down play.

Michigan State played Cover-2, and Hayes was off me a little bit. I set him up with a strong move. I gave him an outside look and went inside. The safety came over, I put my foot in the ground, and Henne put a perfect throw on me; I caught it. There was nothing but grass in front of me, and everybody was going nuts. It was ridiculous. I knew at this point that this was the game winner, so I was going crazy inside.

Michigan State got the ball back but didn't score. We won the game 45–37 in triple overtime. The Ohio State game the year before was my first time beating the Buckeyes and winning the Big Ten. That game was crazy, but that Michigan State game was sick. I've never had that feeling before, and it was the most memorable game for me. It was just on another level.

We finished celebrating and got back to the locker room. We usually came in on Sunday to lift, watch film, and run, but because this game was so long and taxing, Coach Carr told us in the locker room, "Guys, I've never done this before, but I'm giving you the whole day off."

But because we were going to run things differently that year, the seniors said, "We appreciated the offer, but we'd like to still watch film and maybe get a run in. It can be shorter, but we wanted to watch some film."

Everybody got showered up, and as tired as we were, we knew that campus was going to be crazy that night and we needed to go out. We went out that night and partied. We were rock stars. We were gods that night; that's how we were treated. It was crazy because Michigan isn't the kind of campus where cops are lenient toward players. It's not Ohio State, Texas, or USC where you can get out of trouble. I've gotten tickets where cops knew I was Braylon Edwards and didn't care.

That night was different. The cops didn't see anything that night. We didn't do anything too crazy, but the cops wouldn't have cared. I was a celebrity the year before based on what I did, but that night I was like a living legend. It was different. Everywhere we were going it was like, "Oh my God, it's him." We were living it up, too. It was pandemonium everywhere. Whenever I went into a college bar, all the TVs were on *SportsCenter*, and they showed replays of the game all night long. We didn't get tired of it either. They kept the bars open for us, and we just lived it up for that night.

It wasn't just a good night; it was a good week. At this point, I wasn't worried about school either. I was tapped out with school. I was doing enough to stay eligible, and that was pretty much it because I was so far removed from college. I was worrying about where I was in the draft at this point.

We still had a few games left, but that game catapulted me in the conversations for the draft, and I knew it. We beat Northwestern in the next game and we lost to a bad Ohio State team in the last game of the season. Ohio State sucked that year, and we just couldn't put it all together. The game was a weird one where we scored first, and then the second half the Buckeyes were just a different team. They destroyed us, and had we beaten them, we would have controlled our own destiny to get to the Rose Bowl.

We didn't control our own destiny because Wisconsin was playing Iowa, and Wisconsin also had one Big Ten loss. The Badgers beat Ohio State but lost to Michigan State, but with the Rose Bowl, if there's a tie, the team that went last can't go. We went the previous year, so if Wisconsin beat Iowa, it would have gone to the Rose Bowl. We were listening to the Wisconsin-Iowa game on the bus ride home from Columbus.

Iowa won that game, and we were so happy. It happened in just about the middle of the bus ride, so it cheered everyone up. Whenever you're on a plane ride or bus ride after a loss, it's always quiet at first. Then slowly but surely, little conversations get started. Then somebody starts cracking jokes, and then it gets loud, and the coach looks back, and it gets quiet again.

But on this trip, Wisconsin lost, and we cheered and yelled that we were going back to the Rose Bowl. I was excited and was cheering with my teammates, but I knew that this meant I only had one game left in my college career. I only had one game left until we found out if my decision to come back would pay off.

9

Feeling a Draft

MY SENIOR YEAR WE PLAYED TEXAS IN THE ROSE BOWL. I JUST wanted to get out of there with a win. We hadn't won the Rose Bowl in seven years, and I wanted to leave my mark and stay healthy. I didn't pay attention to the pageantry and events. I was focused on going out there and destroying Texas. We went out there in 2003 and 2004, and it was fun. I soaked it all in, and we went to Disneyland. The second time it was a pure business trip. It was a legacy game because this was it for me. I also looked at it as an audition for the NFL.

The Longhorns had Cedric Benson at running back and Vince Young at quarterback. They didn't have any great receivers at the time because Roy Williams was gone. Limas Sweed was young, so he wasn't doing anything yet. Their main offense was Benson and the tight ends. We just had to make Young beat us. The defense spied Young and played zone the first and second downs, but for some reason, Jim Hermann wanted to all-out blitz almost every third down. The first time Young ran for a long gain, I thought, *Don't do that again.* Well, he did and he ended up rushing for 192 yards and four touchdowns on us.

I had three touchdowns and 109 yards, so I had another good game, but we lost again, and this time it was by one point—38–37. I'm not an emotional dude, so I didn't cry that it was my last game. I didn't cry after the Ohio State or Michigan

State games either. I was sad that it was my last game and everything I worked toward was over, but I didn't get emotional over it. At that point I had accomplished a lot of my personal goals. I had become the best receiver in college football and I knew that my next goal, making it to the NFL, was about to come true.

I left the Rose Bowl and, because I had gone through the process after my junior season, we already knew who we wanted to be my agent. We chose C. Lamont Smith from All Pro Sports and met with him at Mastro's restaurant to have a steak after the game. After that I went back to Michigan and then met Smith in Miami, where we flew to the Bahamas, so I could clear my head and prepare for the draft.

After that vacation to get my mind right, it was time to go to work and make sure every NFL team knew that I was the best player—not just the best receiver—in this draft. I went out to Denver to train and I met with Smith, so he could teach me how to answer questions at the combine and instruct me on what I needed to say. I decided not to train with my dad and instead went to Denver because I felt like I didn't want to go back to high school and middle school and deal with that. I felt like the pressure would be on him if I didn't perform well, and that it would be his fault if something bad happened. I didn't want to put that on him. I also got to the point where I didn't want him to be my coach anymore. I liked the father-son relationship that we had formed and I just didn't want to go back and possibly fall back into that relationship we had when I was younger. Looking back on it, I still think that going to Denver and doing it on my own was the right decision.

Smith and I talked about all the mock drafts that were put out. I was a top 10 pick in all of the mock drafts, but on average I was seeing myself pop up in the top seven or eight picks. We started to look at the draft order and which teams had a need at wide receiver. The San Francisco 49ers had the first pick, and they needed a quarterback, so we knew they probably weren't an option. They ended up getting a deal done with Alex Smith before the draft, so we officially knew I wouldn't be the first pick before the draft started. The Miami Dolphins had the second pick that year, the Cleveland Browns had the No. 3 pick, the Chicago Bears had the No. 4 pick, and then the Tampa Bay Buccaneers had the No. 5 pick.

Tampa had just drafted Michael Clayton the year before, so we figured the Buccaneers wouldn't spend another first-round pick on a receiver, especially in the top five. We knew we didn't want to go to Cleveland at three because Cleveland sucks. It's awful; nobody wants to go to Cleveland. It's a bad team. The Browns always have been bad and they don't have a consistent structure in place. They just hired Romeo Crennel, who is a defensive-minded coach. He's a nice guy, but he didn't know anything about being a head coach. They had a new offensive coordinator in Maurice Carthon, and he hadn't had a lot of success in the NFL.

So we didn't want to go there. Lamont didn't want me to go to Chicago, but that's where I wanted to go. He didn't like Chicago because they had Jerry Angelo as its general manager, and the organization didn't like to pay the players very much. I wanted to go to Chicago, though, because it's a storied franchise, a big market, and down the street from Detroit. I would get to play twice a year against the Detroit Lions and could come home every year.

Chicago was really where I wanted to be, but I thought Miami would take me at No. 2, which would mean the Bears wouldn't have the opportunity to pick me. Miami had Gus Frerotte at quarterback, and the Dolphins needed a wideout badly. The Dolphins had Chris Chambers, but he and I would've played well together. So, I thought that Miami was going to be the team that picked me.

I went into the combine with the plan that I wasn't going to participate in any of the events except for bench press and the interviews with the team representatives. Mike Williams was back in the picture with this draft because he was eligible to be drafted. He was a beast in college but had sat out the previous year because the NCAA wouldn't let him go back to school after trying to gain eligibility in the draft after his sophomore season. We knew that Williams had been out and that he wasn't very fast.

Lamont didn't want me to run at the combine because we wanted Williams to run, knowing that he was slow and out of shape. We knew that if he had a bad combine performance, all it could do was help me. I was a top 10 projection. I had all the power at that point, so they told me not to run. I had an ingrown toenail the week of the combine as well, so he was adamant about me not running. The competitor and track lover that I am, though, I was in the hallway of my hotel room the night before the 40-yard dash at the combine, testing it to see if I could run.

But Lamont would have had a heart attack had I run the next day, so I didn't. All I did was the bench press and I did 22 reps. That was a lot for a wideout, but I was pissed because I've done more than that at Michigan. I wasn't doing as much lifting at this point as I was at Michigan, though, because we were doing a lot of speed training so I could perform well in the 40. I wasn't going to run at the combine, but I was going to run at Michigan's pro day. With the spotlight on, that's where we were going to show everyone that I was the best player available.

The only problem was that we didn't have a quarterback to throw at the pro day. Henne was still an underclassman and wasn't allowed to throw, and none of the other smaller colleges had a quarterback that was available. The Dolphins were sending their whole crew out to the pro day. Nick Saban was the head coach and he was there, and Rick Spielman was the general manager and he was there. Steven Ross, the owner of the Dolphins, is a Michigan alum and he was there. Spielman heard that we didn't have a quarterback, so he was the one who threw all the passes for my pro day. This was when we really started to think the Dolphins wanted me because they not only had everyone up there, but their GM was also the one throwing the ball to me at my pro day. I was catching everything and putting on a show. I was getting low on my breaks.

The thing about training in Denver with the high altitude is true. You get more oxygen and you get in better shape with your lungs and muscles. Because of that training, I wasn't having any issues with the work we were doing and didn't feel gassed at all during my pro day. Jermaine Gonzales also did the pro day with me and he was gasping for air. He and I started going back to back on running routes, and when we started running the deeper stuff, I felt good.

I put on a show with the passing portion, but where I really excelled was the testing numbers. I ran a 4.38 and a 4.43 in the 40, I jumped 39 ½ in the vertical. I murdered it, and my numbers blew Williams' combine numbers out of the water. My mom and dad were there, standing by some of the general managers and scouts, and they heard them whispering and gawking about me the whole time. All 32 teams were there because we had Marlin Jackson, Dave Baas, and myself, who all ended up going in the first 33 picks.

I did everything I needed to do, so now it was just a waiting game to see where I would really go. Every day they came out with a new factor of whose stock was rising based on pro days. Ronnie Brown, a running back from Auburn, was nowhere in the mock drafts until his combine because he ran around a 4.4 there. After that he was in the top five. It was typically the same people who showed up in the top five: Alex Smith, Benson, Cadillac Williams, Brown, Pacman Jones, and myself.

It was always a combination of those six guys, so we all thought we would be in that range, but we didn't know the order. Teams started flying us out for meetings, so I went to San Francisco, Chicago, and Detroit. I just drove down the rotunda and went to meet with Lions GM Matt Millen. He and my father are friends, and Millen loved me. I talked to him a couple times in college, and one of the things I had heard was that Millen was thinking about trying to trade up on draft day to come get me.

The Lions were picking at No. 10, but they had just drafted Roy Williams the year before, so I wasn't sure if they would trade up to get another receiver in the next draft. My brother-in-law is Marcus Pollard—he's married to one of my stepsisters—and Pollard was with the Lions at the time. He even said at the time that the Lions had been talking about me and that they wanted me. So it seemed as though Millen was willing to have conversations about trading up for me.

I wasn't sure what was going to happen, but the Dolphins were still showing a lot of interest in me. They were calling, checking on me, talking to my agent. They made it known that they were interested in me. Because they were showing so much interest and saying all the right things, I still thought that's where I would end up—even as we entered draft day.

We went out to New York for the draft, and at this point, we knew that Alex Smith was going to the 49ers, so Miami was basically on the clock. I was sitting in the green room at our table, waiting for Miami to call my name, and I got a phone call on my cellphone. It was someone from the Dolphins asking if this was Braylon Edwards and that they just wanted to make sure I had my phone on me. I was thinking, *okay, I'm going to Miami.*

I already had a condo set up in Miami. That's how far this got. I really thought I was going to be taken No. 2 overall. The Dolphins were now officially on the clock, and the clock kept ticking. We're down to 10 minutes, then seven minutes, but we hadn't heard anything. It got down to two minutes, and I saw Brown across the room picking up his phone. The Dolphins called Brown and drafted him instead of me. I didn't realize it at the time, but all the attention that Miami was showing me was because the Dolphins were angling for someone else to trade up and broker a deal. They wanted Brown the whole time and were working angles with the Washington Redskins and trying to get the Lions to come up and pick me, but they never got any offers they liked.

I started thinking about Chicago at No. 4 because I didn't know if Cleveland would take me. I could go to Chicago, build my brand up in a big city, and still be close to home. That would be good all the way around. Miami would have been crazy because of the city and location, but I can work with the Bears. At least that's what I was trying to convince myself. I was trying to stay positive all the while saying to myself, *Please, Lord, don't make it Cleveland.*

If I would've known this was going to happen, I would've told my agent that I do not want to fucking go to Cleveland. LaVar Arrington did it in the 2000 draft. He told Cleveland that he wouldn't play for the Browns if they drafted him, so with the No. 1 pick, the Browns took his teammate, Courtney Brown, instead. Arrington ended up going No. 2 to the Redskins. Eli Manning did it in the draft the year before me. He told the San Diego Chargers he wouldn't play for them and was traded to the New York Giants.

All of this was running through my mind as I was sitting there with the Browns on the clock. I was thinking, *please don't take me*, and then my phone rang. It was the Browns. Coach Crennel called and said, "This is Romeo Crennel. How would you like to be a Cleveland Brown?" I'm like, *shit, the only Brown I mess with is Charlie*. But it was exciting just to hear my name called and to go No. 3 overall, so I was respectful and happy but nervous at the same time.

This was the dream and something every young football player plays in their mind: being able to walk across that stage after your name is called. My dream of making it to the NFL had come true, and that overpowered any negative thoughts I had against Cleveland. I ran on stage and I think I had the most people ever on stage. We had everybody, including my mom, dad, stepdad, and stepmom, up there. They had been there when this thing started and then they were there with me when the dream came true. I went from that little boy, who watched the NFL intently to bond with his father, to the 12-year-old kid training like an Olympian to a kid struggling to deal with the transition to college to finally an NFL player with the world at his feet. I was the No. 3 overall pick in the 2004 NFL Draft. Every drop of sweat and tears that I put in was on that stage and allowed me to excitedly smile while holding up my new jersey.

I made it. I did it.

That feeling of accomplishment, joy, and relief lasted for a while that day but was quickly replaced by a precursor of what my time in Cleveland would be like. It was raining and snowing pretty bad the night of the draft, so most of the guys who were drafted didn't fly out until the morning. Aaron Rodgers didn't go to Green Bay, and Brown didn't go to Miami. But Cleveland flew me out that night right into a snowstorm. The other guys got to take the *Sports Illustrated* cover picture that night, and I was flying right into a storm. I was like, *this is how we're starting this thing? You're flying me out in a snowstorm in the middle of April?* Everybody else was partying, celebrating, and doing photo shoots, and I was flying into a storm. Little did I know that I was not only flying into a physical storm, but also a metaphorical storm as well.

10

Welcome to Cleveland

IT WASN'T ALL BAD IN CLEVELAND. I DON'T WANT TO MAKE THIS seem like a Browns-bashing session because I have a lot of good memories as a Brown, and a lot of positive things happened while I was there. The Browns were the team that made my dream come true, drafting me No. 3 overall, so I was grateful for that. They believed in me and chose me in hopes that I could help their organization, so once all the dust settled, and my family and I thought about everything, we started to look at it as a positive. I was a top five pick, I was in the NFL, and I was going to be rewarded monetarily for that pick. If I put in the work and did what I was capable of, then everything else would take care of itself.

That plane ride, though, from New York to Cleveland was a good metaphor for what was ahead in my football career. I had never flown on a G5 private jet before, so I was excited and felt good. I had my suit on and was flying to meet my new team. Then we got up in the air, and those little planes take the weather a lot different than a Boeing 737 or a bigger airplane.

The jet was shaking, I saw the precipitation sliding past the window, and all of the sudden, it went from exciting to us feeling like we're in the movie *Airplane!* It was a scary ride in, but we made it to Berea, Ohio, where Amy Palcic, the media relations director for the Browns, led us on a quick tour before meeting with the media.

I walked into the media room, and it was like the media didn't seem too thrilled that I was there. I know their job isn't to be my friend, but I remember feeling awkward walking in the room because of the way they were looking at me. The Browns executives introduced me, and I made my opening remarks. I thanked Romeo Crennel and Phil Savage for drafting me and I promised I would do all that I can. We opened it up for questions, and the first thing a reporter said to me was, "Hey, Braylon, surprised you didn't drive in your Bentley."

I bought a Bentley before I got drafted. I always wanted a souped-up sports car. I had talked to my agent, and we knew I was going to be a top five pick, so I told him I wanted to get one. They asked me not to get it, but I asked if I would be able to afford it. They said yes, so that was my answer. I had that before I was drafted, and a reporter with USA TODAY interviewed me for a story. He came to Schembechler Hall in Ann Arbor, and I happened to drive the Bentley in to the interview. He saw the car and included it in his story, so that became a national conversation. I thought it was behind me, though, but here I was at my introductory press conference, and it was the first thing a reporter asked about.

All the questions were more badgering than they were nice or lighthearted. I was asked, "How do you think you'll help this Cleveland Browns team?"

I responded, "I'm a hard worker. I'm going to roll my sleeves up, and what Trent Dilfer says, goes. I'm going to learn from him. I'm going to learn from the older receivers in Dennis Northcutt and Antonio Bryant. I'm going to give it 100 percent."

I thought I was humble. It wasn't about me; it was about the team, but the reporters followed up by asking, "What makes you say that you can work hard and be humble?"

I was like, "I'm just going to work hard and be humble. I don't understand the question." So it was just an awkward first introduction to the media and my first experience as a Brown. It wasn't the way I was hoping to get my career started.

The next day made it worse because they brought in the top three draft picks: myself, Brodney Pool, and Charlie Frye. Pool was drafted at 20 years old, but he looked like he was 12, and the media looked so excited to ask these guys questions. It was completely different than my press conference. They were throwing softballs at Frye. They were joking around with them, asking Pool about his success at Oklahoma. From the start, I felt this tension between the media and me and I never really understood why.

When I picked No. 17, they asked me why I picked that number. Receivers had just been allowed to take numbers in the teens the year before I got drafted. So everyone went and got the No. 11 because it's the closest thing to No. 1 they could get. I didn't want 11 because everybody else had it. I wanted something with a one in it, though, and 17 was just a number I thought was cool, and nobody in the league was really wearing it.

Once I picked that, everybody said, "Do you know whose jersey number that is?" I didn't know that it was the number of Brian Sipe, who played quarterback for the Browns and was part of the Kardiac Kids in the 1980s. I knew a lot about the NFL from my youth when I studied it to talk to my father, but the one blind spot I had was the Browns. So I didn't know, but the reporters thought I should have known that was a part of their history.

Plus, by this time we had heard that there was some back and forth with the Browns on who actually wanted to draft me. I don't think Crennel wanted to draft me. He was a defensive guy, and Shawne Merriman and DeMarcus Ware were in this draft. I think Crennel wanted to trade down and get one of those guys. We heard that Savage, the general manager, was on the fence, but what pushed it over the edge in my favor was that Randy Lerner, the owner, wanted them to draft me. Couple that information with the way I felt coming out of the media session, and it made me a little leery of what was ahead for me in Cleveland.

Time went on, though, and once we started rookie camp and organized team activities (OTAs), I started to feel more engrained with the team itself. Those OTAs were almost like that freshman year at Michigan, when you're trying to adjust, get in your reps, and find your place. That's when you saw the speed in the NFL. It's not that people were faster, but the difference was people knew what they're doing and how to play at that level. Then, your 4.4 was much faster than someone with a 4.3 who doesn't know what they're doing. Luckily, it was a similar offense to what we had at Michigan, so I studied film, picked up on it quickly, and worked on getting my technique to the level that the other receivers had.

The hardest part about transitioning to the NFL, though, wasn't on the field. It was making friends. In college you're in a concentrated area. And when you finished practice, you had to all walk back to the dorms together. You lived together, ate together, and played together. In the NFL everyone was grown, and some of these guys had families. I had a house, and it's just me in the house by myself. After practice in college, it's like, *what are you guys up to? You want to play* Madden *or get some pizza?* In the NFL it's like, *nah, I have to pick up my daughter from soccer practice, or me and my wife have this and that.* It was just a different situation. You're trying to make friends, but some of these guys are competing with you for their job.

That was a type of adjustment, and, oddly enough, I ended up making friends with some of the fans just because I didn't really know anyone. Some fans consistently showed up to events, sign-ing shows, or golf outings, so you saw some of the same people. I had this group who called themselves the Braylon Bunch. They made T-shirts, painted their van to make it look like *The Brady Bunch*, and I used to have them over to the house for a barbecue. It was probably six or eight white dudes around 30 years old who were always at the events I was at, and I told them one day that I was having people over and that they should stop by. So they did, and it was live. They had a great time.

Up to that point, things were going well. I was adjusting to the game, I had fans in my corner, I found a home, and every-thing was going smoothly. The only aspect that wasn't on the right track was my contract. I had gone through rookie camp and OTAs, and we still didn't have an agreement on a contract, so I was holding out.

I was drafted No. 3 overall, the same spot that Larry Fitzgerald was drafted the year before, so we wanted the same contract that Fitzgerald received in the previous draft. We weren't being offered that same contract by the Browns, though, so my agent went to work, trying to negotiate a fair deal. On top of that, the Browns wanted me to sign a non-compete deal for sponsorship, which I wasn't comfortable with. The Browns had their own sponsors that they worked with, and through this non-compete clause, I would be signing over my rights to those companies. They would have the first rights to sign me to any marketing and sponsorship deals, and I had to accept whatever amount of money they offered. So if McDonald's offered me a local sponsorship for $50,000, but one of the fast food restaurants working with the Browns offered me $30,000, I had to take the $30,000 offer.

That didn't seem right to any of us, and we weren't going to sign anything like that. My mom was big on me preserving the rights to my brand and making my own choices with marketing deals and sponsorships. Plus, there was potential to lose out on quite a bit of money for no reason. My agent and I went back and forth with the Browns management on this deal, and it all came down to the marketing non-compete clause. They offered us the salary and terms we wanted, but they still wanted us to sign this non-compete. It got to the point where I was about to miss a preseason game because they wouldn't budge. Finally, the owner, Lerner, and Crennel got involved and asked what the holdup was. Once they found out a marketing deal was keeping their first-round draft pick off the field, that changed things quickly, and we signed the contract without that non-compete clause. I was free to market myself as I pleased and I was the only draft pick that year to not sign that clause.

I was ready to get to work and for the season to start to show everyone what I was capable of. I had participated in much of training camp, so I felt like I could have been in the starting lineup from Day One. It didn't go that way, though, and I wasn't in that premier starting spot for a few games. The first game was against the Cincinnati Bengals. We started the game in a three-wide-set, so I was in the starting rotation on the first play, but I was the third receiver behind Antonio Bryant and Dennis Northcutt. I still think that was Crennel punishing me for holding out. I always got the feeling that me holding out rubbed him the wrong way. He always talked about earning your spot.

I love Antonio. He was a good friend to me in Cleveland, but I knew I was better than him and Northcutt. That's all I could think about. That first game I only played about 12 snaps, though, and it was a little frustrating because I knew those guys weren't on my level. I was not a quarterback who needs to sit and develop.

After getting drafted third overall by the Cleveland Browns in the 2005 NFL Draft, I pose with general manager (left) Phil Savage and head coach Romeo Crennel (right).

I race past Green Bay Packers defensive backs Joey Thomas (24) and Nick Collins (36) for an 80-yard score and my first NFL touchdown.

In the middle of a promising rookie season, I tore my ACL against the Jacksonville Jaguars on December 4, 2005.

During the early part of 2006 training camp, I rehab and do conditioning exercises while the rest of my Cleveland Browns teammates practice.

I score a 16-yard, toe-tap touchdown against the Pittsburgh Steelers in November of 2007.

We had a lot to celebrate in 2007, including this touchdown score, as we went 10–6 during the last double-digit-win season in Cleveland, and I made the Pro Bowl.

I have my head down, following a disappointing loss to the Pittsburgh Steelers in Week 2 of the 2008 season. I began to grow more and more distant from Cleveland and the idea of being there.

Cleveland Browns coach Eric Mangini, with whom I never got on the same page, talks with me during a 2009 game against the Cincinnati Bengals.

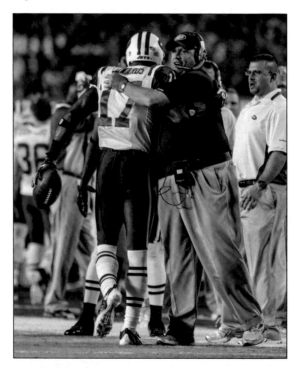

During a *Monday Night Football game*, head coach Rex Ryan, for whom I really enjoyed playing, congratulates me after my first touchdown as a New York Jets player.

After a December 2009 touchdown, I extend my arms in my trademark Jet Nation celebration.

Defensive back Darius Butler tries to take me down during our 28–21 playoff victory against the mighty New England Patriots, following the 2010 season.

re an 80-yard touchdown during
FC Championship Game loss
e Indianapolis Colts.

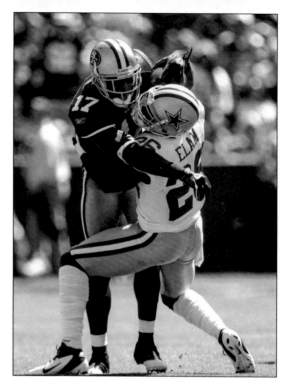

I injure my knee on this play against the Dallas Cowboys in 2011, and that injury led to a deteriorating relationship with Jim Harbaugh and the San Francisco 49ers.

I catch a pass for the Seattle Seahawks during September of 2012, my last full season in the NFL.

My mom, Malesa Plater, is my biggest supporter, as well as my business manager and a great source of advice. *(Malesa Plater)*

I wave to The Big House crowd in 2016, as the Michigan program remains close to my heart.

I'm a wide receiver. I thought, *throw me the ball and tell me which guy to block on the play, and I'll go get it.*

The next week was a whole different experience because we went to Lambeau Field to play the Green Bay Packers. I was a little off before the game because you're out on the field at Lambeau, and Brett Favre was out there warming up. Having been a kid who had studied the NFL and watched the league intently, it was a little shocking to see Favre on his home turf that close and in person. That was a special moment. But the pregame warm-up made everything feel real, and once I got that first hit in the game, it all clicked back in, and I got into game mode.

I didn't start that game either, but Northcutt dropped about three passes in the game. He dropped a slant that would have been a nice gain, and Crennel told me to get in the game and replace him. I was so hyped up from being in Lambeau and then I was in the top two, replacing Northcutt. I needed to make my mark. Packers cornerback Joey Thomas was covering me and trying to talk trash, saying stuff like, "Okay, we got Mr. First Round over here." I just thought to myself, *this dude doesn't know what's about to happen.* It was a blocking play, and I picked this dude up, drove him into the ground, and jumped on him. He ran over to the ref, yelling, but it happened near our sideline, so no one else was saying anything to the ref. You could see everyone's eyes were wide open, like did you just see what he did to that dude?

Later in the game, we called a play where I run a slant. I saw the corner jump outside, so I jumped inside, and Dilfer put the ball on me for an 80-yard touchdown. A touchdown at Lambeau Field! It was incredible. I got to the sideline, and everyone was going crazy. I finished the game with three catches, more than 100 receiving yards, and a touchdown, but more importantly, we won the game.

We played the Indianapolis Colts the next week. The third overall draft pick just helped you beat Favre and the Packers. You didn't play him the week before against Cincinnati and you got demolished. But once again against the Colts, I was still the third receiver. We lost that game to the Colts, and the media was starting to pick up on the fact that Crennel wasn't really playing me. The coaches and the players were starting to pick up on it, too.

In Week Four against the Chicago Bears, I was set to get more reps. I still wasn't starting, but I had more plays coming to me. I also noticed, though, that my right elbow was agitating me. It wasn't hurt, but it was hot, which usually means it's infected. Monday went by. We're off Tuesday, we had a good practice on Wednesday and Thursday, and Friday was a light practice. We had our walkthrough on Saturday.

I woke up on Saturday and I had a Popeye arm. My forearm was swollen like I've never seen, and it's still hot, so I knew something was wrong. I went to the training room to see our trainer, Marty Lauzon. He and I got close because I had a strained groin during rookie camp, and I went to him to get stretched out that whole camp. I showed him my arm, and Lauzon downplayed it and told me to go through the walkthrough. Afterward he said he'd take me downtown to Cleveland Clinic to let the doctors look at it.

We got to the hospital downtown, and I could tell that Lauzon downplayed it. I could tell that it was more serious than he was letting on. The doctors looked at it and they told me I had a staph infection. Cleveland had a rash of staph infections from 2005 to 2008, but I think this one happened during the Colts game. I thought maybe the rubber pellets in the turf bounced up and got rubbed into a scratch on my arm, which wasn't uncommon.

The doctors told me they needed to operate on it, drain it, and I'd have to stay in the hospital until it's completely drained. I was just about to get more playing time and then I had to miss the game against the Bears. You can't play around with staph infections, so they kept me in the hospital for a few days and then made me sit out any team activities for a few days once I was out of the hospital.

I had to get stitches, I missed the Chicago game, and then I was pissed because we're about to play the Baltimore Ravens, and Deion Sanders still played for the Ravens at this time. I was going to get to play against Prime Time and I had to sit out because of an infection. I was happy I wasn't seriously injured, though, so it wasn't an issue to come back and get into the swing of things.

The whole season Crennel was playing games with me like we're in high school. He wasn't starting me, saying I needed to earn a spot. I don't know what else I could have done to earn that spot, but we made it to the Miami Dolphins game in November, and this was a twofold game for me. The Dolphins screwed me in the draft, and because they screwed me, I'm now in Cleveland dealing with Crennel's games. So I had a lot of motivation in this game.

The first play of the game was a slant. I caught it behind me, spun around Zach Thomas, and took off for about 40 yards. I had one pass where I jumped over Northcutt, caught it, fell off his shoulder, and ran for another 15 yards. I didn't score in the game, but I had six catches for about 90 yards. I was showing them this is the kind of player I was, and that if they put me in the game, I was going to make plays. I was happy with how I was practicing, happy with the effort I was giving. All I wanted was seven to nine looks a game. If we had a running back that was killing it—by all means—run the ball. I'd throw some blocks, break some plays open, but we didn't have that. I should've been getting the ball.

Part of that was the coaches' decision to not play me very much, but part of it was the quarterback situation. Dilfer was the quarterback up until the Jacksonville Jaguars game, but at that point in the season, Frye was now going to start and lead us. I loved Frye. He was a nice person. He was funny and cool. At that point it was over for Dilfer. Frye was young, had moxie, and could throw the ball.

I was excited, too, because let's just say that Dilfer and I bumped heads. When I first got to Cleveland and gave that first press conference where I said I was going to learn from Dilfer, follow his lead, be humble, and work hard, Dilfer cut out all the quotes from a newspaper story about it and posted them in my locker. They put my locker right next to his, so the first time I met him was right after I saw all the newspaper clippings in my locker. He walked up to me and said, "I'm going to hold you to all this. You said all these things. Nobody asked you to say it, and you said all these things." I told him I said those things because they were true and that I hoped he would hold me to them. I didn't just say some bullshit just to say it. So Dilfer looked around and said, "Woo, you're snappy for a rookie. Hey, we got a feisty rookie."

"Women are feisty," I said. "I'm aggressive." I was ready to go out and be the best I could be. Plus, the last time I checked, the Browns hadn't made the playoffs in a long time.

He said, "It's always the rookies, always the guys who thought they knew something." That's how we started right off the bat in OTAs. Right before he got replaced by Frye, he said something to the whole team along the lines of nobody in this room knew what it's like to be a champion. Nobody knew what it takes to get to that point. Everyone was like, *so because you rode the coattails of arguably the greatest defense ever, now you know something?* He was a first-round draft pick, too, just like me, so he should have known what I was coming in to. Even though he had been in my shoes, he worked against me. And there was no reason to be intimidated. I played a position that would help him.

In the Jaguars game, I scored a touchdown on a Hail Mary because the defense was offside. I just ran, and Frye threw it, and we scored on a 45-yard touchdown pass right before the half. I caught another one on a zig route. I thought that this was about to be the beginning of something, that we were building some chemistry, and that we had something going with Frye at quarterback.

In the fourth quarter, I noticed that Jaguars defensive back Rashean Mathis was jumping everything. He was taking a lot of chances, so I told our offensive coordinator, Maurice Carthon, that we should run a hitch and go. I ran that route, but Frye had to avoid a sack and threw kind of a floater, so Mathis was able to catch up to it. I jumped up and caught it. It was one of those situations where my right leg was supposed to be the dominant leg, so the left leg relaxed. My right leg got caught on Mathis' foot and slid out, so my weight never came down. When my left leg finally came down, I tore my ACL. I knew it was bad immediately.

I was frustrated that the injury happened, but I thought that we only had four games left and we weren't going to make the playoffs anyway. It would've been nice to build on that chemistry with Frye, but I'm a strong person and I'd get back from this. I asked Lauzon that if we got surgery right away how long it would be until I was ready to go. He said if we did it the right way we could get it ready full speed in probably four months.

I rehabbed, let the swelling go down, and then had the surgery on January 2. I knew I would be able to come back from that and I knew that no one would be able to come in and replace me, but I still needed to come in and do my job. I went out on a bang, too. I had five catches for 86 yards and two touchdowns against the Jaguars. So if I got right again, Kellen Winslow came back, and you paired us with Frye, we could have something. There was some hope in the air about what was happening, so my goal was to have the fastest rehab I could. I told the trainer to push it until he thought I shouldn't go any further. That *Rocky IV* theme music, which Charles always used to hum, was playing in my head again.

At first, it was tough. It was snowing outside and cold, and all I was doing was rehab, icing my knee, and more rehab. I was stuck in cold Cleveland with limited mobility and nothing to do. Finally, around March, my knee was doing a lot better. I was walking without hearing a clicking sound and had pretty much my full range of motion, so I told the Browns that I needed a little time to get away.

It had been nothing but cold weather, so I took Mike Hart, my cousin, and Morgan Trent down to my condo in Miami. We had some fun in the sun, hung out in some clubs, and played football on the beach. I had my knee brace on, so I was trying to be smart about it. I shouldn't have been playing in the first place, but I did have the brace on. If the ball came to me, I just pitched it to Hart or Trent, and they ran with it. But the ball came to me on a kickoff and instead of pitching it, I bolted. I shook one guy, another tried to tackle me, and I jumped over him. I got in the end zone, and everyone was like, *Dog, are you supposed to be doing that?* I felt good, though. I had some swelling that night, but there was no pain.

Once I got back to Cleveland, I saw Lauzon and said, "Marty, you'll never believe what happened." I told him how we played football in the sand, that I felt great, and that I felt like the knee was getting to 100 percent. He looked at me and said, "Don't do that. We're on a good plan. Let's stay on the plan and not reinjure it." He reminded me that the season wasn't until September, so we had a lot of time left to get it right, but that also meant there was a lot of time to reinjure it as well.

I heard what he said, but I was pushing myself and trying to get this thing right as fast as I could, too. I wasn't doing anything stupid, but I also wanted to make sure I was doing as much as possible to get back to 100 percent. Normally, we would play a lot of basketball after spring ball to stay in shape and for a good workout. I was hurt, so I wasn't supposed to be playing, but I went back to Ann Arbor for a weekend to visit with Hart, and they were about to hoop. At this point, I was jumping, running, and squatting in rehab. I was squatting more than I ever had because I was always running track at Michigan when they were going through the weights program. My legs were as strong as they had ever been, and I was feeling great. I went to the court with Hart and Hayes Grooms, who was my good friend. He was a walk-on basketball player at Michigan and would eventually become my manager.

Grooms was usually by the book; he didn't waver off the line too much. He was worried about me and told me I probably shouldn't be playing basketball. I told him I was good, that I had my knee brace on, and that I would be smart about it. About six minutes into the game, I was yelling for an alley-oop from Grooms. I saw the reluctance in his face, but he threw it up anyway. I went up and got it. And to be totally honest, I had never jumped that high in my life. I went up, got it with one hand, and slammed it in. Everybody was looking around, thinking, *what did they put in his knee?* It was like a bionic knee.

I immediately called Lauzon, and he asked me if I was playing basketball. I said, "How did you know? Are you psychic?" He said he heard the basketballs bouncing in the background and told me that I shouldn't be doing that. But I told him what happened and that I had never felt this strong in my life. The knee was fine and it didn't move or bend or anything when I landed. He told me he was glad that I got that out of my system because he knew it's human nature to want to test it and make sure the knee could handle that type of activity—but that I better not do it again.

That time I listened and didn't play basketball again that summer. I felt like God, or the universe or whoever, gave me that moment to tell me I would be all right and that I probably shouldn't test it again. I stayed in Cleveland for the summer and started planting, cutting, and blocking. The Browns eased me into training camp and then held me out of the first three preseason games as a precautionary measure. I played in one quarter of the fourth preseason game.

I took my knee brace off before the game and then ran a slant against the Buffalo Bills—and former Ohio State Buckeyes— Nate Clements and Donte Whitner. I caught the pass, and Whitner went up under me and flipped me up a little bit. My leg was in the air, and Lauzon saw from the sideline that I didn't have my brace on. I ran over to the sideline, and Lauzon looked at me and said, "You're going to kill me." I told him I was fine and I felt great, but I could tell I was still playing a little timid because I was nervous about hurting it again.

I was fine. I just wasn't used to playing with an injury that severe, but we made it to the opening game against the New Orleans Saints. The first play of the game, I told Frye if the safety came down, I was going to sell the corner real hard, so he could just let it fly and I would get it. I motioned across and I saw out of the corner of my eye that the safety came down. I gave the corner a hard outside stick and slid off his inside shoulder, and Frye threw it 75 yards for a touchdown. This couldn't have been a better way to start the season. The last time the fans saw me, I was being carted off the field. The only problem was the left tackle was called for holding, and the touchdown was negated. The air went out of that building, but I think more air went out of me than the stadium. We ended up losing that game, and it was a precursor for that 2006 season.

We went 4–12 that season. In the NFL guys were conditioned to realize what type of team it's going to be real early on in the season. And we noticed early on that year that it was just not going to be our year. Some guys took themselves out of it, especially guys with families. Early in the season, if you're in it, the energy was up, and guys were cracking jokes. Guys got to the practice facility early. But if you got late in the year and you're losing, it's cold outside, and guys were arriving 15 minutes before meeting. If you knew you're out of the playoff hunt, you started talking about different things. Guys started talking about taking a cruise in February or a vacation in late January.

I tried to never be like that, but guys knew early on whether it was going to be a good season or not. Guys weren't giving up, but they're checking out. If the season wasn't going their way, some created elements of injuries. It started with little nagging ones so they didn't have to practice but could still play in the game. Some of them have played long enough that they knew terminology and what they could get away with. And they'd know the terminology from having used a chiropractor, a trainer, or a massage therapist. They milked that knowledge to get out of practice. I saw that in 2006 because it was my first full season.

The 2007 season, though, was different. We had Derek Anderson come in at quarterback when Frye got hurt. Anderson was always a cool, funny guy and he had a rifle for an arm, so we were all optimistic about what he could do. We had Winslow back and we added Joe Jurevicius, so we thought we would be good in 2007. And that season was different. We all felt like everyone was on the same page, humming on all cylinders. Anderson was tearing it up, Winslow was Winslow, and it was the best I had felt since college. It wasn't just wishful thinking. We thought people were in trouble when they played us.

The season was also different for me because I got a little perspective halfway through. After we beat Miami, we were 3–3 and had a bye. I got a phone call from Palcic, and she said there was a local high school boy who was sick. He had a heart transplant, and it recently started failing, so he wasn't doing well. She said I was his favorite player, and he wanted to meet me. "Say no more," I said. "I'll be there."

I went to the hospital, and he was hooked up to wires. He was only 16 years old. Here I was a football player with everything I asked for, and he's 16 years old and fighting for his life. It wasn't fair and it struck me in a very powerful way. I spent some time with him and his mom in the hospital. I held his hand, and he looked up at me as much as he could. Before I left I told him that I was dedicating the rest of the season, especially this next game, to him.

That next game was against the St. Louis Rams, and it was probably the best game I've ever had. I had eight receptions, 117 yards, and two touchdowns, but every play was great. I caught a touchdown sliding on the ground. I ran a go route and caught it with one hand while getting two feet in. I caught a slant and ran the safety over. I took my helmet off and started yelling at the crowd once I got up. Every play that game was special, and it just felt like I had an extra gear in that game. We won 27–20, and I went back to the locker room and got cleaned up. Then Palcic came over and told me that the boy had passed away. They had known that he died Saturday night, but they didn't tell me until after the game was over. I went and spoke to the family and gave them some tickets to another game, but I was heartbroken.

I'm not an emotional person, but I cried after hearing that news. Why did I deserve to be in the NFL, and he deserved to die of a failed heart transplant at 16? It put a lot into perspective for me. I had dedicated my entire life to sports, and maybe there's more to it than that. We don't appreciate people in our lives, and it's about more than money and having a nice car. It was an emotional shock to my system at a time when I felt like I was on top of the world and, quite frankly, invincible.

This came in a year when I made the Pro Bowl, and our team finished the season 10–6. We had a ton of optimism toward what was ahead, but it was something that still sticks with me today. It just wasn't fair. That changed something in me, and I was about to find out that there would be more change happening very quickly around me in Cleveland.

11

From Romeo to Mangenius

THAT 2007 SEASON REALLY WAS MAGICAL FOR ME. I KNOW WE didn't make it to the playoffs, but we were getting better. I made it to the Pro Bowl, and it seemed like there was legitimate hope for what we were building. We saw fewer people going to the trainer with those nagging injuries that season. Instead they really were contributing and holding their own weight, which helped build morale for the whole team. Once we finished the 2007 season, we were all excited to get to work on 2008, but that excitement quickly faded as everything started falling apart pretty quickly once we got into the preseason.

Derek Anderson and I were clicking in organized team activities (OTAs), we're riding the momentum from the year before, and I was coming into my own in terms of peak strength and knowledge of the game. This was the first time we had the same offense in place, so I had a real comfort level there.

We played the New York Jets in the preseason, and I had a one-handed touchdown against Darrelle Revis, which was exciting. But then that next week, all the receivers ran to cool down and stay in shape after practice. The Browns brought Donte Stallworth in from the New England Patriots, and Stallworth was a good friend of mine since college. We met when Michigan played Tennessee in a bowl game, and I actually helped persuade him to come to Cleveland. I told him to look at what we did last season, that we needed another receiver like him to help, and he decided to sign with us.

We ran after practice, did over-and-backs, and I always took my shoes off to run to let my feet air out and breathe. I was ahead of Stallworth, beating him in the runs, and he decided to run from behind and jump on my back. When he did that, his cleat slid down my leg and gashed my leg open. This wasn't just a small scrape or cut. They cleaned it out with saline solution, and you could see my Achilles. It wasn't cut deep enough where it hurt my Achilles, but it was deep enough to have an open wound.

Cleveland was so nervous about staph infections that they sent me home for the next two weeks, so I sat at home and did nothing for two weeks. The media picked up on that and added their two cents once we got into the season, and I dropped some passes. They somehow related the injury to us doing horseplay and not taking things seriously, which wasn't the case. I was just running ahead of him, and he decided to jump on my back.

But at that point, I was used to the media treating me that way—from the first press conference to 2006 when I decided to go to the Michigan-Ohio State game in Columbus. It was No. 1 against No. 2, and they had moved the game from noon to 3:30 PM because Bo Schembechler had passed that week, but I still thought I would have enough time to make it back to the team hotel for the team meeting at 8:00 PM.

We had a game that Sunday, so we always had a team meeting Saturday night. Since the game was in Columbus, I decided I could take a helicopter from Cleveland to Columbus, stay at the game for a while, leave early, and make it back with plenty of time to spare to get back to the team meeting. It was only about a 45-minute helicopter ride, so I thought it would all work out. We went to the game, watched it, and ended up leaving with about nine minutes left in the fourth quarter. We probably stayed a little bit too long, but we were still good on time because we were going to land right in downtown somewhere close to the hotel.

I had Amy Palcic, the media relations director, ready to pick us up once we landed, so she could take us right to where the team was. Unfortunately, it happened to be a cold night that night, so we couldn't fly the helicopter back. Instead they sent a small airplane, but the plane had to de-ice before we could take off. We're sitting on the plane for 15 minutes waiting to de-ice, and the clock was ticking. I was starting to get nervous about the time now because this was 15 minutes we didn't account for, and we already knew we should have left a little sooner than we did.

We finally took off, landed in Cleveland, and Palcic was waiting outside for us. We jumped in the car and booked it to the team meeting room. We got to the hotel at 7:58 PM, I ran through the doors and down the hall and finally made it in the meeting room, but it's 8:05 PM. I was five minutes late. I was not super late, but as Lloyd Carr always said, "if you're early, you're on time. If you're on time, you're late, and if you're late, you're forgotten." So I heard that in the back of my mind and was thinking, *here we go again*. I knew I was going to hear about it.

Add in the fact that I was dressed head to toe in Michigan gear—I mean, I had on this big ass Mike Hart jersey, a Michigan hat, maize and blue Nike Presto's—and was walking in looking like a Michigan billboard. It was also a small room, and I was trying to walk in quietly. Romeo Crennel saw me and he could've let me sit down, but he called me up to the front of the room. He said, "Since you went to the fucking Michigan-Ohio State game, you come up to the front and sit." He made me sit up front, finished his talk, and broke us up into position groups. Terry Robiskie was our wide receivers coach at the time, and his son,

Brian, went to Ohio State. So Robiskie just looked at me, laughed, and said, "Fuckin' Braylon Edwards, I fuckin' love you."

I lost a ton of money on that game because Michigan lost. I won $78,000 at Greektown Casino the week before the game. I gave the money to my financial advisor and told him to put all of it on Michigan. No spread, no points. Had I taken the points, I would've won, but I lost that. Anyhow, it was No. 1 against No. 2. I wasn't going to miss that game. I was five minutes late, but at the Browns game the next day, I had the best game I had as a Brown to date. I had seven catches for 137 yards. We lost, but I played my ass off. After that game reporters came up, and the first thing they asked about was me being late for the team meeting. They said, "Sources say you went to the Michigan game and arrived to the team meeting late."

I told them, "I'm here to talk about Pittsburgh. We took a tough loss, and if you want to reconvene tomorrow and talk, I will."

The first thing they asked me on Monday was about me being late. I said, yes, I was at the game, but because our airplane had to de-ice, I was five minutes late. The only thing I would have done differently was just left earlier than we did. If it wasn't for a snitch in the locker room telling the press about it, we wouldn't have even had that conversation. Had I been benched or it impacted how I played, then fine, that's the media's job to find out why I didn't start the first half.

In the 2008 offseason, I was in my Bentley with a female celebrity. We were coming back from the club, and I was going about 120 mph. We were almost to the exit on the freeway that would get us home, and a cop came out and flashed his lights. It was a long drive home, and he got me right before my exit. I told my passenger to act like she was sick. I told her to put her head in her lap and pretend she was as sick as a dog.

The police officer came up to the car, asked for my license and registration and why I was going so fast. I said, "Officer, I'm sorry. This young lady is very sick, and I didn't want her to throw up in my vehicle. I didn't want to pull over to the side of the road because that's not always the safe thing to do." He looked at me and asked if I was Braylon Edwards and told me that I had signed a football for one of his cousins who was sick. He looked at me, looked at my license, and told me to get her home but to slow down.

He let me go without ticket, but about a week later, I got a call from a reporter with Channel 19, one of the local news stations. She said, "Braylon, what's this I hear about you going 120 in your vehicle, and you didn't get a ticket?" I told her I didn't know what she was talking about, but she told me that the police officer had taken a picture of the radar gun that read 122 mph and sent it out to a few people. One of the people he sent it to happened to work for Channel 19, so now that got out, and the media reported that I was speeding.

Because the story got out on the news, the Avon Lake police department was embarrassed that I didn't get a ticket, so they sent a police officer to my house and had him issue me a ticket for speeding. I deserved the ticket, but the whole thing just showed how the media was always there next to me, meddling in everything I did. They somehow knew every little thing that happened to me and—even if it didn't impact my performance on the field—they nitpicked me.

We never got off on the right foot—at least that's how it always seemed to me. That was one of the biggest differences between Cleveland and some of the other places I played. Even in New York, where everyone thinks the New York media is terrible, they treated me different than the Cleveland media did. In New York they cared about the bottom line on the football field. If you did something incredibly stupid or incredibly great off the field, then they would care about that, too, but I always felt they were fair with me.

That 2008 season began with the media and even some fans talking about how Stallworth and I were horsing around, and it was a precursor for the whole year. I recovered from that preseason injury and didn't miss any games and I remember I was one of the few starters to play the whole season. D'Qwell Jackson was a younger guy, but he started that whole year, too. That might have been it for the bigger name players because Kellen Winslow got hurt that year. In 2008 I played with five different quarterbacks.

We started off with Anderson, and then Brady Quinn took over. Quinn got hurt, and Ken Dorsey took over. Dorsey got hurt, and Bruce Gradkowski came in. Gradkowksi got hurt, and Josh Cribbs had to play quarterback at the end of the season. It was a rotating door at quarterback, which made it difficult for the whole offense. I struggled with drops that year, and it was back to that old feeling that we just weren't going to do anything productive. I got used to Anderson and the way he threw the ball, and then Brady Quinn threw this mean ass knuckleball, and then Dorsey, who has no speed at all on his passes, was throwing. Gradkowski threw a spiral, but he was about 6' tall, compared to Anderson, who was 6'6", so it was tough for him to throw over the offensive line.

It felt like we had the rug pulled out from underneath us after that 2007 season and how much momentum we had coming into 2008. I think that made it even more frustrating because we felt like we could've done some damage, and it all just fell apart in one season. And Cleveland will turn on you quickly. We went 10–6 in 2007 and then 4–12 in 2008, and everybody forgot about the playgrounds we built around the community, or the foundation we started to give tuition to local eighth graders. All the good stuff went out the window, and it was about me dropping the ball.

It all spiraled down very quickly for us, and the Browns fired Crennel after that season, which, looking back on it now, was putting the cap on what would amount to my time in Cleveland. It was pretty shocking to see us collapse that quickly, but we were professionals and had to move forward. After the Browns fired Crennel, they brought in Eric Mangini, and I just never got on the same page with Mangini.

In terms of a football mind, I think he is one of the most brilliant guys there is. I haven't been around Bill Belichick, I haven't been around Bill Parcells or Bill Walsh, but from what I've seen, Mangini knows every aspect of the game. Sometimes a coach will say something to you and you're thinking, *you've never played wideout. I'm not listening to you.* I overlooked that with Mangini because he knew the game so well.

One-on-one he was a great dude. If you talked to him by himself in the office, he was great. But when he got you in front of the team, he called guys out, kicked guys out of meetings, and just didn't know how to handle the team the right way. When Mangini was hired, I was in Miami, so I didn't get to meet him right away. I called my boy, Kerry Rhodes, who played for him in New York. I asked Rhodes what was up with him, and Rhodes said he was so glad that guy was gone from New York. That set a bad tone for me going into it, and it was only reinforced once we actually started team activities and OTAs.

Mangini had this thing where he wanted you to remember everyone's name. He asked a veteran guy, Eric Barton, in training camp to stand up in a meeting and name all the wide receivers. Barton got my name and one other guy and then he looked at Mangini and said, "75 percent of these guys won't be here tomorrow, so why do I need to know their name?" Mangini said, "Good answer, now I need you to leave the meeting, and you're not practicing." He would call cats out like that.

On the field he would start practice over. It didn't matter where we were at in practice. If something happened that he didn't like, he would start the whole thing over. This wasn't college. I was a grown man, and you didn't restart practice after an hour and a half of us working out. Some of those guys had kids to pick up.

Mangini had us doing tackling drills, but everybody had to do the drills. So I was out there playing a running back and getting tackled by guys who might not even be on the team. I was the No. 1 receiver, so why were you letting me get tackled by someone who might not be on the team? I went through once, got up, threw the ball down, and said, "I'm not doing this again." He looked at me and told me I needed to pick the ball up because I was going to go again. He kicked me out of practice and called me into his office afterward.

It wasn't just one thing with him. It was a bunch of little things that piled up and it rubbed everybody the wrong way. On top of that, we started that 2009 season in a big hole, so tensions were high, and nobody was happy. After we lost to the Baltimore Ravens, which dropped us to 0–3, Mangini was mad about the loss, came in on a Monday, and said if anyone wanted to leave this team, they should see him in his office and he'd see what he could do for you. I was the first person in his office. I told him the Browns weren't going to win. It didn't matter about Mangini coming in, Crennel, Jesus, or Santa Claus. Cleveland's not going to win.

Free agents didn't want to come here, and he wasn't going to change the culture. He asked me about the 2007 season and said we beat a lot of teams that year. I told him we beat a bunch of bums because every team we beat that year had a losing record. I told him I was tired of being here, that it was my fifth year, and that I was ready for a change of scenery. It was obvious that our relationship wasn't going to get any better, and I just felt that my time in Cleveland had passed. He said, "All right, we'll see what we can do."

Then we fell to 0–4 after we lost to the Cincinnati Bengals at home in overtime. It made it even more frustrating because we just couldn't win a game. Nothing was going right, and after that talk with Mangini, I grew more and more distant from Cleveland and the idea of being there. Everything started to get old to me, and I had that anxious feeling that I just needed to get out of there.

Even our routine that we went through started to get old. After losing a game, we would all go downtown to this club called View. We went out, everybody got drunk, forgot about the game, went home—lather, rinse, repeat. We were losing so much that it was just the same thing one week after another. I wasn't used to losing like this. I had never lost that much in my life and I was trying to manage that with not getting along with my coach and not really having my mom, dad, or stepdad right there to help me or give me support. I was in a bad place mentally and just wanted out.

When we were at View after the Cincinnati loss, I decided I was ready to go. Hayes Grooms was there with me, and I just looked around and saw my whole career flash before my eyes. This was going to be the rest of my career if I stayed in Cleveland: go to practice, work hard as shit, play the game, get beat, then go to the same club every week, and act like the game didn't happen.

I told Grooms I was about to dip, gave him my card to pay for the bottles, and that I was pulling the car up around the front. He asked me what was up, and I just told him I was tired of everything. I went outside, and the party promoter for View was outside. His name is Edward Givens, but everyone calls him Duck. He saw me leaving, and Duck asked me where I was going. I said, "Man, I'm just over it. I'm tired of losing, and this shit is whack." When I said that, I pointed at the club. He's the promoter of the club, so when I said that, he took it personal.

He looked at me and said, "Man, you whack." I was like, whatever, nobody has time for your short ass. Then he said, "As a matter of fact, I always thought you were whack. You a clown."

He had two dudes on each side of him. These five guys started to circle up on me. I'm from Detroit. I'd been on the playground and I knew what's about to happen to me. Either I was swinging first or I was getting jumped. This wasn't a situation where we're all just going to walk out of it, and everything was going be fine kind of deal.

So I hit Duck, knocked him out, knocked out another one of their boys, and took off. I jumped into the car of the Cavs' No. 1 draft pick, J.J. Hickson, because he was there, and we were friends. He took me over to my car. I jumped in my car, swung around, and picked up Hayes and told him what happened. He said, "Man, you didn't have to throw a punch." I told him he wasn't out there and didn't see what I saw. They were about to jump me.

The next morning Mangini called me, and I told him what happened. He told me not to talk to the media, to tell them it's a police investigation, and they'd figure it out. I talked to the media that day, and the media made Duck out to be LeBron James' best friend. Duck was an associate of James. He was friends with a guy named Rich Paul, who is really close to James and now his agent, so they were friends, but they weren't best friends or anything. Duck spun the story that I was some jealous individual, and I always just said it was a police investigation. I let them deal with it and then I said I would talk after that.

Then the media went and interviewed James that day, and I don't know if he wishes he could take this back or just doesn't care, but his response was that it was childish on my part. He said Duck was super small, and it was almost like beating up his son. This was 10 years ago, so his son was about three years old then. Then James said, "Braylon has always been a jealous individual, so maybe it just came out. I don't really know." I was like, *a jealous individual?* We played in the same city, drove the same car, both had families that loved us. I was confused.

But I never said anything in public about it because it wasn't worth it. I was made out to be the bad guy. And because I wasn't talking, all they had was Duck's side of the fight. He came out and said I had teammates there holding me back, which wasn't the case. He went to the hospital and told the doctors he was having concussion-like symptoms and got a doctor's report. Then he went to the police station and got a police report, so I knew immediately that he was going to try to cash in on this and try to get himself a payday.

I wasn't at the hospital, I wasn't at the police station, I wasn't at the scene, so Duck's story became the bible. I hired an attorney almost immediately because we knew what was coming. We went to court and we went back and forth on whether or not we should settle or push forward with the case. I knew I didn't do anything wrong. They tried to jump me and they got beat. Montee Ball, the former Wisconsin running back, went back to Wisconsin almost a year after my fight and got jumped. He got beat up, though, so he didn't get in trouble. I got jumped, but I won the fight, so now it's an issue.

I was telling my attorney and my mom that we should take it to court and push forward. My attorney said once we go to court there were no limits to what they could bring up. They could look at my entire past, how many times I was in the club, how much I was spending. They would try to drag me through the mud and make me out to be an even worse person than they were already trying to frame me as. Because of all of that, my attorney advised us that we should go to civil court and settle, and my mom agreed. I felt that was an admittance of guilt, but Mom is always right, so that's what we did. I had to pay $150,000 for getting jumped.

That all came out on Monday, and on Wednesday I got a call from Mangini. Coach called me in and said, "I wanted to let you know: we traded you to the New York Jets. I think it'll be a good move for you, a good place for you." I couldn't get out of Cleveland fast enough. I was so thankful that trade happened.

But because of the timing of the trade and the fight, the narrative became that the Browns were tired of my distractions, that the fight was the last straw, and that James had some influence in me getting traded. Nobody knew I asked for a trade a week before that. I wish Coach Mangini could have said something about the fact that we had some conversations in the past, that I wasn't happy, and that they were trying to work on something, but it didn't happen.

I don't know if the fight factored in to why they traded me or not, but I know that there had already been talks, and they started to throw feelers out there. The Browns had drafted Mohamed Massaquoi and then they drafted Brian Robiskie. They had a new offensive coordinator and a new wide receivers coach, so Mangini might have wanted to see if we could all be a three-headed monster at receiver.

Either way, I was happy I was traded. It seemed like bad timing back then, but looking at it now, the fans had started to turn sour on me because we had a bad season again. I was frustrated and starting to get close to checking out mentally and I didn't know how I would have handled another season and offseason there.

I understood the frustration from the fans because we felt it as players, too. The fans placed all their expectations and hopes on the big-name players. If bad things happened, it's our fault. I had a bad season, I dropped some passes, and that's all Cleveland fans remember. Even to this day, I can read a comment on social media and know exactly what state the person lives in based on what they said. It's unfortunate because the ideal situation would have been to have great success as a Brown, win a ton of games, and make those fans happy. It didn't turn out that way, though, and New York was going to be the fresh start that I needed.

12
New York, New York

AS MUCH AS I WISHED IT HAD WORKED OUT IN CLEVELAND, I WAS so happy to be heading to New York. Outside of Miami, New York was a place that I spent a large amount of my free time. I love New York. I spent time there shopping, eating, partying. It's such a great place.

When I was sitting in Eric Mangini's office, and he said they were moving me, it was like it was in slow motion. I saw his mouth move and heard him say "New," and he didn't even have to finish it. I knew he was about to say New York. I remember thinking to myself, *oh my God, he's about to say New York.* I was actually thinking it would be the Giants and that I'd get to go play with Eli Manning.

Then he finished the sentence and said the New York Jets. I was so happy to leave Cleveland that I just said, "Yes, the Jets, I love it." I honestly had no idea what was even going on with the Jets or what their team looked like, but I didn't care. I left his office and didn't even go to my locker to get my stuff. I had a laptop, a speaker, cologne, pictures there, but I didn't give a fuck. I was out of there as fast as I could move. On the way out, some of my teammates passed by me and said, "What up, B?"

I was like, "Just got traded, man. See ya later." I grabbed Josh Cribbs, D'Qwell Jackson, and Andre Davis and said good-bye to them, but that was about it. We were 0–4, the fight happened, and it wasn't against anyone else, but I just wanted to get out of there as fast as possible.

I got in my car, and it just hit me. *I was headed to New York!* I started playing Frank Sinatra's "New York, New York," screaming it at the top of my lungs. From October to January, my voicemail recording was: "start spreading the news." My mantra became "Doing It My Way." I'm a very opinionated, strong-willed person. I'd rather do it my way and fail and figure out why I failed than listen to advice. There have been a lot of times where this method has burned me, but I stick by it. I'd rather feel the success of doing it my way. It's just always the way I looked at things. That's who I am.

Once the initial excitement wore off and I came back down to earth, I realized I still knew nothing about the Jets. When I realized that they were 3–1 to start the season, I was like, *holy shit, I'm going to a 3–1 team.* I didn't even know what 3–1 felt like. I was screaming Sinatra again, just ready to take on this new challenge in my favorite city and be a part of something great.

I hopped on a flight to New York, put on a suit, and all the guys on my new team clowned me because I had a suit on. But this was an audition for me. I was under contract, but this was my last year with a team option year after that, so I was trying to get that option picked up and then hopefully a new contract after that. I wanted that first impression to be great and impactful.

They were doing team pictures when I got there, so I jumped out of my suit and started to throw on the team colors. In my excitement to get out of Cleveland, I forgot what colors the Jets had: green and white. I was like, oh man, not the green and white. It felt weird to put that on because I will always associate those colors with Michigan State. Of all the colors, it had to be green and white. I would've preferred scarlet and gray to green and white, but I was cool with it as long as I was in New York.

We had a press conference after the pictures, and this was really the only part about this new beginning that I wish I would've done differently. Because the media still wanted to know about the LeBron James issue and the fight in Cleveland that didn't stay in Cleveland. They asked why I had an issue with James and what happened. I told them I never had an issue with James and that I thought he's a phenomenal talent, a great player, and great for the sport of basketball. Then after that, I said it's a legal matter, and it's going through the justice system right now.

I wish I could do that whole thing over. My mom and my lawyer can kiss my ass. I would've told the New York media, "Listen: I was outside the night club, and Edward Givens and his boys were about to jump me. It didn't go so well for them, I beat their ass, and now I'm getting sued because I'm an athlete and can improve his status. I don't care how small Edward Givens is. It's four on one, and y'all lost the fight. It was four guys. They surrounded me, and before they got the chance to attack, we got into a tussle, and I was the man on top in the end."

That's what I would've done because then you would've had my story and you would've had two sides. You wouldn't have had to believe my side, but at least the two sides would've been out there. That was the only regret or negative to that beginning, though, and once that passed, I was ready to get rolling.

We had Mark Sanchez at quarterback and Rex Ryan as the head coach. Ryan was with the Baltimore Ravens when I played in Cleveland, so I saw him twice a year. He was very aware of my capabilities because I used to trash the Ravens defensive backs, Chris McAlister and Samari Rolle. McAlister was known for being a wild apple and he was across from me in one game, playing man coverage. This was during a game, and I could smell alcohol on McAlister's breath. More specifically, I smelled Hennessy. I've been around Hennessy enough that I can smell it, and he had a reputation for being around clubs the night before games. I got back to the sideline and told my offensive coordinator, Rob Chudzinski, that McAlister was still drunk. I told him I smelled alcohol on his breath and told him to call a go route. I told Chud I'd run it lazy and make it look like I was blocking and then I'd put my foot in the ground and go. Chud said, "Are you sure?"

I said, "Call it."

We called the next play, and McAllister was so lost. I didn't even do anything and blew past him. So Ryan had seen what I could do, and I knew what Ryan had done defensively with the Ravens, so I was excited to work with him. On top of everything else, my first game with the Jets was a Monday night game. I'm traded to New York, it's my favorite city, and now we're about to play Monday night. I couldn't have scripted this any better.

I practiced like a man possessed, and it worked out for me because Sanchez was a young quarterback who they were trying to ease in, so the playbook was easy. I had to catch on quickly to get in the next game, but I went to Michigan. I had two offensive coordinators there and four coordinators in the NFL. I had learned six systems from 2001 to 2009, so whatever you threw at me, I was going to get it.

And I had only been there for a short time, but I already knew the Jets had someone on the roster who was going to push me and make me better. Going up against Darrelle Revis in practice was like going up against Marlin Jackson when I was at Michigan. We were going to sharpen each other and help the team at the same time. Revis was the type of guy where if I got him in one-on-ones or practice, he would say, "Hey, come back and show me the move. How did you get me on that? All right, run it again." Ryan would be like, "Well, you heard the man," and we would run it again. We were competitive like that. We went at it.

That relationship would continue throughout my time in New York, but it was something I noticed immediately when I got there. It helped get me ready and get in the right mind-set that this team was going to compete for something important and that we had something to play for. I wasn't used to that, so I needed that mental shift. That helped me prepare for that first game, too, because I was nervous.

It's Monday night. All eyes were on us. We went down to Miami, went in the locker room, and put the pads on for the first time. I put the green and white on for the first time. Mike Tirico was calling the game, and he's an Ann Arbor guy. We're about to take the field, and I was still nervous. I hadn't been nervous like this since my first game at Michigan. For me, it was like everyone was focused on me and this trade. I was nervous, but I also knew this was my chance to shine and show everyone that I wasn't a cast-off.

When we were in the huddle in the first quarter, that's when I knew the Jets were going to be a good fit. Sanchez called a play on the second drive, and I scored a touchdown in the back of the end zone. We ran this play in practice and knew it would work. We scored, everyone was excited, and the nerves just melted away with that score.

That gave me some confidence for the rest of that game and showed that I belonged there and I could help this team win. Later in that game, we got a penalty to make it third and 20. We're in the huddle, and Thomas Jones was talking. We had the who's who in New York at the time. We had Jones, Nick Mangold, Alan Faneca, Tony Richardson, Jerricho Cotchery, and Damien Woody, and everyone was talking in the huddle trying to get us back on track. I looked around and I just yelled out, "Shut up. Just throw me the ball."

I just got here. This was their team, and everyone's looking at me like, *who the hell is this guy?* Sanchez called the play, looked at me, and gave me a look like it's coming to me. He dropped back. It was Cover-2, and this was a good play for that coverage. The throw was one of the prettiest throws I'd ever seen in my life. He threw it, I caught it, and we scored. I got in the end zone, but the refs reviewed the play and called me down on the 1-yard line. They said my knee was down before I broke the plane and called me down. It was definitely a touchdown. I still believe that today.

But even though they overturned it, I got us down to the one and I knew this was going to be a good thing. We lost the game, but I still knew it was going to be a good season. It was a strange feeling because everyone who had been on the team before I got there had their heads hung because of the loss. We were now 3–2 and just gave up a game we probably should have won. But it gave me some confidence and pushed out a lot of bad thoughts that I had circling around my mind.

I finished the game with five catches, 64 yards, and one touchdown after basically just a week of being with the team. We, as humans, naturally let doubts sink in to our heads. Even though I asked for a trade in Cleveland, I started to think about how the Browns actually went through with it. *Did that mean they didn't want me? Am I that bad of a player? Can I still do it with a new team? Am I no longer a No. 1 wide receiver?* My head was in such a different space after that game. All those negative thoughts were squashed by that performance. I had to hide that excitement, though, because we just lost. I couldn't show my excitement until I saw my parents, my manager, and my sister after the game.

It was just a different feeling with the Jets. Practices were different. Walking into the building was different. The game was different. In Cleveland the games felt like: how are we going to lose this one? There you walked into the building, and it was just different. New York had this state-of-the-art facility in 2009 with glass, chrome pillars. It was a modern look that just felt good to walk into. You walked into the facility and you saw Joe Namath and pictures of all the greats who had come through New York. You saw a Super Bowl trophy staring at you, and that impacted me. You saw it in the building, and it became doable, something you could achieve, too. It's like when I went to Michigan. You walked through the trophy room, saw the Heisman, and thought you could do it. It's the same thing when you walk in and see that silver trophy. Later when I was with the San Francisco 49ers, I saw five of them. San Francisco had them right when you walk in the facility, right there waiting for you. You saw those every day to remind you that you needed to be great today.

I was ready to be great for the Jets and felt fully acclimated after that first game. Unfortunately, we lost the next game to the Buffalo Bills and couldn't get a win in my first two games. Sanchez had a bad game against Buffalo, and they already didn't really trust him throwing the ball yet since he was still a young quarterback.

We had a traffic light play system for him. Plays in the red meant that's the play and that he couldn't audible out of it. On amber light plays, Sanchez could audible to one other play, and that's it. Then there were green light plays where Sanchez could do whatever he wanted.

I was fine with that because I loved to block. I learned that through George Sahadi at Bishop Gallagher High. I wanted to make my presence felt. Plus, as a wide receiver, you have to find ways to make the game fun if you were not getting the ball. Terrell Owens said it perfectly when he was with the Dallas Cowboys. They didn't throw him the ball the whole game and then they threw him a big ball in the fourth quarter, and he dropped it. He said don't avoid throwing me the ball for three quarters then get upset that I dropped it in the fourth. I tuned out a long time ago. I wouldn't say it like that, but T.O. is absolutely right.

Not many people know this, but for wide receivers and corners, there's a lot of talking going on during games. Not trash talking, but actual conversation. If there's a good defensive back that I respected, I started talking about his family and offseason plans. I was really good friends with Champ Bailey. So the play would be going on, and I'd ask Champ if he was still doing his big barbecue over the summer. That wasn't just me; it was every receiver and corner.

But I didn't mind blocking and waiting for Sanchez to get more comfortable with the plays until they would open things up a little bit. Plus, Ryan was a players' coach, which made it easy to play for him. He let us be us. As long as we were operating between the guidelines, he was good with whatever. Eric Mangini wanted to control every move. When I was with San Francisco, Jim Harbaugh wanted every second to be accounted for. Ryan didn't need us to be there until nine at night every day. He understood that football wasn't everything. Some guys had kids, were married, and just like any other job, we wanted to go home and enjoy our lives. Ryan was great from that aspect.

So even though we didn't win those first two games, I was still good with what we were building toward and the whole situation. I knew it was a matter of time before we started getting on the right side of the win column. We beat the Oakland Raiders, lost three in a row after that, and then won three in a row. We lost to the Atlanta Falcons to drop us to 7–7. We beat the Indianapolis Colts because they rested some of their players for the playoff.

We were 8–7 going into the game against the Bengals, and Cincinnati had already clinched a playoff spot. We thought we were probably out of the playoff picture because a lot had to happen for us to get in. We ended up beating the Bengals and we got the news in the locker room after the game that we actually made it into the playoffs. I was losing my shit in the locker room because I had never made it to the playoffs before.

We got into the playoffs and in the first round we got to play Cincinnati, who we just beat 37–0 to close out the regular season. Sanchez had gained some confidence because we were 5–1 in our last six games. Ryan was great about keeping practice the same and consistent, so went in confident and beat Cincinnati for a second time in a row.

We beat the San Diego Chargers in the next round to set up a matchup with the Indianapolis Colts in the AFC Championship Game. Before we got on the plane to go there, I thought about what this meant. Just a few months ago, I was 0–4 and in the worst space of my professional career. I just got into a fight, and the city of Cleveland and I were bumping heads. Then I was one game away from the Super Bowl. I called my agent at the time and thanked him for this deal because I had never been this happy in my life. Obviously, my time at Michigan was better, but Michigan was a means to an end. This is what it was about. Michigan was a step to get here. I love Michigan, I wanted to be great at Michigan, but I wanted Michigan to get me here.

Heading into that AFC Championship Game, we approached that week a little differently. We approached it as if we were going to the Super Bowl. Ryan said that after we beat the Colts we'd have an appreciation day and then a practice. He had printed out a schedule—as if we had beaten them already—to get it in our minds that we could do it. We had a good gameplan and really thought we were going to beat the Colts.

That whole week was crazy. We were talking to friends and family about how we were going to go to the Super Bowl. I wanted to make it to the Super Bowl to stick it to Cleveland. I was planning on just going dumb in the Super Bowl. I even had my MVP speech all written out and practiced and everything. I was going to say, "I want to thank God for putting this on me, blessing me with this ability. I want to thank my mom, dad, my sister, I love you guys. I also want to take the time out to thank the Cleveland Browns for being dumb enough to trade me to this amazing organization. Hey, I guess I can catch a pass." I was practicing that speech when we beat Cincinnati.

But we played the Colts, and they put a stop to that speech ever making it to the light of day. We forced a turnover right before half. We were up seven with about three minutes left and after the turnover we thought we could put a nail in their coffin before half. Our offensive coordinator, Brian Schottenheimer, played it to run the clock out and get a field goal instead of going for their throat. Since we were getting the ball to start the second half, they thought we could play it safe, get the field goal, and get the ball right back. So we ran the ball, got in field-goal range, and then Jay Feely missed the field goal. We gave Peyton Manning the ball back with 53 seconds left, and I had never in my life seen an execution of the clock like he did that day. He put on a clinic, and they scored within 30 seconds.

We went into the locker room up three and about to get the ball back, but you would have sworn we were down 40 points. We were just so demoralized by how that first half ended. We came out flat in the second half and we just weren't the same for the rest of the game. Both of our running backs got hurt, and I had 100 receiving yards in the first half but finished the game with 100 yards. We lost the game and lost our shot at the dreams of playing in the Super Bowl, which was devastating.

We were upset, but we still knew we had a great team for next season. The only problem for me was that I was a restricted free agent and was waiting to see if the Jets were going to pick up my last year on my contract. I loved it there, so I was hoping everything would work itself out. Luckily for me, there were no issues, and my agent called and said the Jets were picking up the contract year.

After that I trained hard. This was the first time I trained with my team the whole offseason, and I went after it to try to build on the last season. I was optimistic about the way we were training, and then on top of that, we signed Jason Taylor, LaDainian Tomlinson, Antonio Cromartie, and Santonio Holmes. I thought we were going to run through the AFC.

It was funny that we signed those guys, too, because I hosted Holmes and Cromartie on their recruiting visits at Michigan. I had a perfect record hosting recruits. I hosted Steve Breaston, and he ended up coming to Michigan. I hosted Lamarr Woodley, and he came. I hosted Jake Long, and he came. Jason Avant was another. My track record was great, but the only person I didn't get at the time was LenDale White. But he'll tell you to this day that I was the best host. He was a Cali dude, so he wasn't going to come to Michigan, but he had a good time.

Holmes' visit was straightforward. He was a good kid, quiet. Cromartie's visit happened after my sophomore year, and his was not very straightforward. On his visit Cromartie was talking shit the whole recruiting trip. He said, "If I come here, you're going to be the second receiver. Marlin Jackson, he ain't that good. I'm gonna play both positions."

I looked at him and said, "Dog, you're not that good. You're some skinny country kid that's going to come up here and get your mind blown. You need to take your ass to Florida State because you're going to come up here and get hit up under your chin and you'll have to figure out what day it is."

He was talking shit to me. *A high school kid talking shit to me, the No. 1 jersey at Michigan?* Needless to say, we didn't get Cromartie at Michigan. But I was cool with both of those guys, and adding them to the Jets was a big deal because we had just found out we were going to be featured on *Hard Knocks* on HBO. We watched it, but we had so many celebrities on that team that there wasn't enough camera time to go around. It was all right and cool. It wasn't a big distraction or anything we thought about. So we didn't pay a ton of attention to it. It was just more cameras around us. We already had so much going on: the Revis holdout, Ryan's personality, Tomlinson, Taylor, myself, Bart Scott, Nick Mangold, Kris Jenkins, Sanchez. There were so many personalities and moving parts, and it was New York. It wasn't like doing the Cincinnati Bengals where you have two stars, and you had to search for storylines.

In a matter of six to nine months, I had gone from 0–4 and a frustrating situation in Cleveland to New York and playing in the AFC Championship Game. Then, I re-signed for my sixth year, and we signed the Monstars from *Space Jam*. We got through organized team activities (OTAs) and mini-camp with the new additions, and everyone was thinking the same thing. There's going to be some problems for our opponents. Looking at the AFC, I thought we should've beaten the Colts in the playoffs last year, and they were dwindling. The Patriots were beatable, but they still had Tom Brady. The AFC could be ours.

The energy around our organization was so positive—even in the community. I remember I went to a Jay-Z and Eminem concert at Yankee Stadium, and the energy there was flowing. People were excited about the Jets for the first time in a long time. I was running into people that loved the HBO show, that loved the Jets. I saw Mark Wahlberg one night and Vin Diesel in a nightclub. Everyone was just excited to see what we were going to do that season, including us.

Highs and Lows

THE EXCITEMENT HAD BUILT AROUND THE CITY, AND WE WERE ALL just ready for the 2010 season to start, so that we could unleash on our opponents. The exposure and hype increased with the first game because it was a Monday night game, and it was against the Baltimore Ravens, Rex Ryan's old team. Unfortunately, our bubble was popped, and we lost the opener 10–9 to the Ravens. We just couldn't get anything going and just had a bad game. We bounced back, though, by beating the New England Patriots in the second game to get some of that excitement back. That quickly faded after that game for me personally, as I was about to have some legal trouble.

Jerricho Cotchery had a charity poker event and he had been asking people to come out to it. We got out of meetings late on Monday that week after the Patriots game. Usually, we finished Mondays around 1:30 PM, but this time we didn't get out until around 5:00 PM. Cotchery's event started at 6:00 or 7:00 PM, so it was going to be a close call to make it on time. I always got a driver in New York. As I said in court, you can check my American Express as it related to a particular driving service and you'd see this service on there repeatedly. It was a car service with four cars in the fleet owned by a guy named Tito Sanchez. I never drove in New York if we were going out because I just didn't like driving there, and it was usually a far drive.

Since we were so late getting out of the meetings, by the time I would've been able to get Tito's service to pick me up in New Jersey, I probably would've been too late to get to the city. So I decided to drive out to the event. I parked my car and went to the poker event. After it was over, I drove to the area we would be going out at and barhopped from there. We went to Del Frisco's for dinner, two other spots, and then to a nightclub called Butter.

We left Butter around 3:00 AM, and I had D'Brickashaw Ferguson and Vernon Gholston with me. They parked back at the poker event. I told them that I wasn't even drunk and that I could take them with me. I realize everyone says they're not drunk when they get a DUI, but I felt that I could drive and was fine to take them. Ferguson and Gholston are some of the most responsible guys I know, so they wouldn't have let me drive them if they thought I was messed up or couldn't drive.

We jumped in the car, got on the highway, and started making our way home around 3:15 AM. I was in the far right lane and I noticed a cop was in the far left lane. I saw him at the first light and thought nothing of it. Then at the next light, he moved over one lane. And then the next light, he's right behind me. Sure enough, his lights went on, and he pulled me over.

He came up to my vehicle and told me the reason he pulled me over was because the tint on my windows was too dark. I didn't do anything else wrong. He looked around the inside of the car and said he smelled alcohol and asked if anyone had been drinking, and I said I had one or two but nothing crazy and that the passengers had been drinking. He asked me to get out of the car and told me he was going to give me a breathalyzer test. Normally, they're supposed to wait 15 minutes after pulling you over before submitting the breathalyzer, but he had the tube out of the plastic wrapping and had it ready to go right when I got out of the car. I blew in it and registered a 0.12 blood alcohol level. The legal limit was 0.08, so he handcuffed me and took me to jail.

I don't think he knew who I was, so it wasn't a case of profiling. I think he was just trying to get somebody and I happened to be there. At this time, everyone was still excited about us, and we were coming off of a win against the Patriots, so we were the team everyone was rooting for. The cop brought me into the station, and all his co-workers looked at him like, *what the hell are you doing? That's Braylon Edwards.* He still didn't seem to know who I was, and it didn't mean anything to him, so he put me with the general population and then moved me to my own cell after about 45 minutes.

I wasn't necessarily upset, but I was just thinking about where this was going to go. Was this going to be private or was it going to hit the media in a big way? The last incident I was in with the fight in Cleveland seemed to be a big deal, so was this going to be much of the same? I started thinking about the worst that could happen, but I was also telling myself that I did everything right. I didn't resist. I cooperated with the police, and there wasn't an accident. So it shouldn't be that big of a deal. I convinced myself it would be fine.

My attorney, Peter Franklin, came to the cell around 9:00 AM to talk to me about what would happen next and what we needed to do. He wanted to get me in front of the judge late in the day so there would be less media around. He felt that if we were in front of the judge early that day that the media would make a spectacle of it, so I didn't get out of the cell until around 3:30 PM. I had almost been in there for 12 hours, just sitting with my thoughts.

Franklin talked to the press, I apologized to my mom, and we finally went back home. I knew I needed to talk to Rex and the

Jets. We had been in the AFC Championship Game last year, were on *Hard Knocks*, so the spotlight was already on us, and then this happened. Everything was going in the right direction, and now there's a negative mark on us from something like this. The media asked me about it, and I handled this differently than the LeBron James stuff. I told them, "it is a legal matter, but at the end of the day, you already know from the police reports. My two teammates are responsible, and I don't think either of them would've let me drive if I wasn't capable of driving."

I just wanted to get back into the routine and get back to the season because winning would cure all and help this go away. If we could keep winning, the questions wouldn't be focused on me anymore and would go back to the team, which is what I wanted. Ryan benched me for the first quarter of the next game against the Miami Dolphins. It was a big game because it was a divisional opponent, but I said I would take my lumps and I did. I took it like a man and didn't say anything. I stood next to Ryan the whole time and then I started the next quarter. My first play was a 67-yard touchdown catch. We're back, and the DUI was erased temporarily from the minds of everyone watching. Success always cleared everything, and we went on a five-game win streak to get off to a 5–1 start. The excitement was back after that first loss and after the DUI.

Despite the fact that we were winning, the only problem was that I think I started to see that we actually had too much on the roster. You have me, wide receivers Santonio Holmes, Cotchery, Brad Smith; running backs LaDainian Tomlinson and Shonn Greene; and Dustin Keller at tight end. Offensive coordinator Brian Schottenheimer was all over the place trying to appease everyone. He was trying to feed L.T. the ball to get him his yards, and I always felt like he wanted Holmes to have success there, so they got him as many balls as they could. Holmes was suspended for the first four games of the season because of his second marijuana offense. When he got back for the Minnesota Vikings game, instantly Schotty went back to feeding him the ball. I was going to be a free agent after this season, so I felt like Schottenheimer was featuring Holmes to get my stock to drop so they could afford to sign both of us for the next season.

Mike Tannenbaum, the team's general manager, and Joel Segal, Holmes' agent, were good friends. So I think those guys were trying to plan something the whole time. As soon as Holmes got in the game, Schottenheimer got him the ball. I started in 16 games that season, and Holmes played in 12. I had 904 yards and seven touchdowns on 53 catches. He had 52 catches with 746 yards and six touchdowns in four less games than I. We were winning, though, so during the season I didn't let it bother me. As long as we were still on the right track and I was putting up numbers to get a new contract, then I was good.

I got to go back home to play the Detroit Lions, which was a fun game. We ended up beating them and were now sitting at 6–2 on the season with our next game at Cleveland. It's the first time I headed back to Cleveland, and I couldn't wait to play the Browns. I was on a winning team, we're rolling at this point, and the Browns were 3–5 coming into this game. I just knew I was going to go off and have a crazy game. In my head I was thinking 170 yards, two touchdowns, and me throwing my helmet in the crowd or something crazy. I got myself so hyped for that game and went out and had a mediocre game. I had four catches for 59 yards. We went to overtime but got the win. That was what mattered.

The game didn't go as I expected in terms of my production, but it was still intense. The fans booed me while I was on the team in Cleveland, so you can only imagine the things I heard now that I wasn't on the team. When I went out for warm-ups, oh my God. I loved it, but every curse word you can think of was directed at me. They called me a loser, and I laughed because we had a winning record and were headed for another win.

I actually surprised myself because I thought I was going to go in and talk a ton of trash and get into it with the fans and media, but I kept it professional. After the game I was asked by the media about coming back and how it felt. I said, "You mature in life, and I felt that I just came here to play football. I was focused on our goal of winning a game and doing whatever it took to help the Jets, and that was it."

I kept it above water because I realized it just wasn't worth it. I had moved on, and they moved on, so I thought it was best to just go our separate ways. It didn't help that my numbers were just decent in that game. But it was mainly that I just didn't want to go out like that. We won and moved on to the next game.

Eventually, we got to 9–2 and ran into a buzzsaw against the Patriots. They beat our ass 45–3 on *Monday Night Football*. We didn't even watch the game film afterward because it was so bad. Ryan took us outside the facilities that week and buried a game ball in the dirt. He dug up some dirt and buried it as if to say we were burying that game, and it was over and done with. That's how bad we got beat. Burying the ball didn't work very well because we lost to the Dolphins the very next game. But we got through the season and finished at 11–5, which meant we were back in the playoffs. All we needed was to get in and we did it.

We played the Indianapolis Colts in the first round and we owed them some payback for beating us last season in the AFC Championship Game. They snuck in after the 2010 season. They won their division, but their division was terrible. We beat them by making a field goal at the end of the game and ducked out with a close win.

Then we had to go back to New England for the second round after getting whooped by the Patriots about a month earlier. We had a good gameplan this time around and we ended up winning 28–21. I never talked trash during it because I didn't get the ball enough. We beat the Patriots the first time in the season, got destroyed the second time, but we knew we were better than them. With the second game, we got in a hole early, our offensive playcalling was bad, we didn't bounce back, and we tuned out. It was one of those games. The next game we went back to the playbook that worked the first time and were more aggressive. The defense took it personally, and we went out and beat them. That win was a big one for us emotionally and mentally because of the way they beat us in the regular season and because it was the Patriots. Holmes and I were literally doing backflips after the game because we were so excited. We got a little too excited, though, because I think we got stuck in that week and that win and we got beat by the Pittsburgh Steelers 24–19 the next week.

Troy Polamalu didn't play in the regular-season game because of an injury, but he played in the AFC Championship Game. He still wasn't 100 percent, and we knew he was still injured, but Schottenheimer felt like we had to change the whole gameplan because of Polamalu being back. He was just in one spot the whole time, but we ran away from him, and they ended up beating us. We lost again in the playoffs, and as much as I loved New York, I was starting to get fed up with Schottenheimer and his playcalling.

I wasn't under contract anymore once the season was over. I was hoping to get a new contract, but my free agency came at the worst possible time. The NFL went into a lockout, and

I was without a new deal. That's the worst time to be a free agent because everyone was getting lowballed since there was so much uncertainty around everything and what would happen. We weren't allowed to have any team activities, so I went back to Michigan for the offseason and gave up my place in New Jersey. Mark Sanchez held a camp in Mission Viejo, California, and I went to the camp to show that I was a part of the team and I wanted to be there with the Jets. But I didn't have a deal, so I was wondering if the Jets wanted me back.

We went from January to around June without headway, and then they finally opened up the lockout, allowing us to start team activities again. I spoke with Tannenbaum and told him I was heading to Cleveland for the final court date for my probation from the fight with Edward Givens. That was my last hearing, and nothing else was getting added, so I thought I was good with everything.

The day I went to court in Cleveland, Tannenbaum signed Holmes to a new deal for five years and $50 million. I don't know why, but they paid above and beyond what they had to pay him. Because of the lockout, everybody else was lowballing players. He and I worked well off of each other, so I thought they would want both of us back. Plus, Holmes already had two slipups with the league, so if he messed up again, he would be suspended for the whole season. He had his second strike that past season, and it was a risk to only sign him and not me. I was willing to take less to stay because I loved New York, so this was a big slap in the face. I felt like they could've paid both of us $5 million a year, but I knew based off of what they gave Holmes that they weren't going to sign me.

That was one quiet car ride back home from Cleveland. Here I was in the city I was trying to get away from and I found out the city I loved didn't want me anymore. I was pissed, my mom was pissed, my dad was pissed, and my manager was pissed. I drove the whole way back in silence just looking out the window because I knew it was all over.

I didn't know what would happen next. I knew I had a good year from a production standpoint. I thought I would get a deal somewhere, but I just didn't know where and for how much. The only thing I knew for certain was that I wouldn't be playing in New York. I tried not to think about it too much after that and just let my agent do his job, but we weren't getting very many bites. It was still slow because of the lockout, and I think some teams felt like they could get a good deal if they didn't show their cards right away. I was getting antsy, though, because it was July and I still didn't have a deal. So I started talking to some guys I knew around the league. Kerry Rhodes was still one of my good friends and he was now with the Arizona Cardinals. John Lott was also with the Cardinals at this time. He was the strength coach for a few years in Cleveland and he was also at the combine, so I had known him for a long time. I was talking to Rhodes, and he was telling me they needed someone opposite Larry Fitzgerald.

I reached out to Fitzgerald, and he asked me if I was ready to come out to Arizona and ball with him and I was like, hell yeah. Ken Whisenhunt was the head coach at the time, and Fitzgerald told me he reached out to Whiz, who said everything was good. Lott called me and asked me if I was ready to go, and things picked up really quickly. It all happened so fast. It went from Rhodes and me talking about the potential to the general manager actually putting an offer on the table. It was a Saturday, I was at a pool party, and my agent told me there was a deal for three years, $24 million, and a $15.5 million signing bonus. I was ecstatic to get offered a deal, but more so because I had some stability again in what was a really unstable time in the NFL.

I was ready to go, ready to be a Cardinal, and was probably going to go out there and sign on either Monday or Tuesday. I decided to relax on Sunday, the day after I found out about the deal because I knew that the coming week I would be putting in work and getting my body in shape for the season. I decided to go out on my boat at the Detroit Yacht Club with some family and friends and party a little bit. We stayed out there for a while, and my boys and I decided that we were going to go out that night to get one last night in. My mom looked at me and told me not to go out. She said, "You guys had some drinks on the boat, you had fun, just go home."

I told her, "No, I'm going to go out because I have to fly out in a few days and get going."

I should have known that Mom is always right, but I didn't listen, and we went out that night in Birmingham, Michigan. We're at the bar, and there was a dispute between my table and the table next to me. It was getting close to the end of the night, so I was having a conversation with one of the guys at the other table, and we decided to just squash it, and everybody had fun. By the time security comes over, we had already smoothed everything over, and it wasn't a big deal.

But security came over again and riled everybody back up. I was done with it. I was ready to go home, so I stepped out of the booth I was in to get away from it. A close family friend was with us in our booth. His brother also was in the front of the club and wasn't even there with us, but he saw the ruckus and he came to the back of the club all riled up.

The busboy came up to us acting like he was a security guard and started getting into it with my friend's brother. They're about to fight now because this busboy was acting tough toward him. I asked security if I could go into the kitchen and just hang out until everything was done because I legitimately didn't want anything to do with this. Security said no at first because they were going to start funneling everyone out the front door and said that I would be fine. Then I had to sit there watching these two idiots—my friend and the busboy—go at it. These were the two most non-important people in this bar, and they're starting the fight. I told them to chill and tried to get in to break it up, and the busboy looked at me and said, "I'll beat your ass, too." I was trying to be peacemaker; what the hell was he talking about?

I could tell this was getting out of control so I grabbed a security guard and told him I was going into the kitchen to get away from this. I was just standing in the kitchen, texting on my phone when the busboy angrily stormed into the kitchen. He didn't know I was in there at first, but then he locked eyes with me, grabbed a broom, broke it over his leg, and then started running at me with this broomstick. He went to swing at me. I ducked, scooped him, slammed him on the floor, and hit him. The security guards saw that it was happening through the push doors to enter the kitchen, so they ran in to break it up. When security rushed in, my friends saw them coming in, so they followed security and tackled them. My friends, for whatever reason, then decided to stab the security guards with a fork and a knife.

Everything got broken up. I left the club, and my friends got arrested because they just stabbed the security guards. I wasn't in any trouble, though, because I was only protecting myself when the busboy charged at me. I was so mad at my friend because none of this would've happened if he didn't come over and get into it with the busboy. To this day our families are no longer close.

196 • Braylon Edwards: Doing It My Way

When my mom found out about the fight, she looked at me and said I told you so. The next morning all the media outlets picked it up. It hit the wire, and Arizona pulled its offer. A $15 million signing bonus was gone like that. Once Arizona pulled the offer, my mom got me, my manager, and a guy who worked for my foundation all at the house. She had us all on the couch and cursed us all out. She laid into us as hard as I've ever seen. She had me crying because I went from uncertainty to stability back to uncertainty again, and it was my fault.

That's a hard pill to swallow. All I had to do was not go out—like she told me—and I would've had another team to play for and another contract signed. Knowing that deal was on the table, I should've gone home. I should've taken it out of everyone else's hands and just gone home. That's not what happened, though, and now it's part of my story and part of what shaped my NFL career. To think I could've been lined up on the other side of Fitzgerald with a three-year deal, and it was gone in an instant because of some clowns causing trouble. It still haunts me thinking about it. It was August, and I was back to square one, trying to find a new place to play with the hopes that someone would just take a chance on me.

The Last Stand

LOSING THAT DEAL WITH THE ARIZONA CARDINALS MEANT THAT I was back to not knowing if another team would pick me up, where I would be playing ball, or even if my career was coming to an end. I wouldn't say I was depressed, but after that whole process, those thoughts were starting to creep in of what's next. It reverted back to high school when I was trying to get my offer from Michigan. I had already shown what I could do, I had some bumps in the road, but I showed I was a valuable commodity, and that offer still wasn't coming in. That feeling was familiar, and I knew it eventually worked out at Michigan, but the NFL is a whole different beast.

That's why I felt such a rejuvenation after the Cardinals offer and an even bigger letdown when it fell through. I earned another chance and then let it all go. But, luckily for me, it was only a matter of days before I was contacted by a new team after the Arizona deal was off the table. The San Francisco 49ers called and expressed interest. The home of my favorite wide receiver, Jerry Rice, was calling to set up a deal. I had spoken with Rice before and was excited that the 49ers wanted to talk, so we flew out, and they offered us a one-year deal for $1.3 million with incentives that could get me up to $3.5 million. It was a far cry from the $15 million signing bonus I could have had in Arizona, but it's another opportunity and another job.

The deal from Arizona was pulled on Monday, I was in San Francisco on Tuesday, and the 49ers called me on Wednesday morning to offer the contract. It all happened very fast. But since there were no mandatory workouts in the offseason, I didn't work out as hard as I should have. When I signed the deal with San Francisco, I wasn't the type of athlete I had been in the past. I wasn't going into camp in great football shape, which put me behind where I needed to be. That was a small concern for me in the back of mind, but I was also thinking about the year I just had in New York. I killed it in 2010. My numbers might not have been eye popping, but I was so efficient. I had one drop the whole year, blocked well, and put up the numbers I did even with the Jets featuring Santonio Holmes more than I.

I looked at the San Francisco roster and knew that Michael Crabtree was injured, so there was an opportunity for me to come in and contribute and make a name for myself again. I said to myself, *it's a one-year deal, it's San Fran, I'm going to play hard, and then we can reconvene next year.* I went in with the right attitude and the right focus mentally, but my body just wasn't in the right shape.

Without that lockout I think I would have gotten a deal a lot quicker than I did rather than waiting all the way until August. But that was no excuse for me being out of shape. I should have done more and after I had a deal and was headed to training camp I was regretting not putting in the right work. I had to use training camp to get into shape. And I usually came into training camp in peak physical condition. Back in the old days, guys did use training camp to get into shape because they had other jobs, but that doesn't cut it now. Guys are in amazing shape now by the time camp starts, and I needed to catch up to that.

Everyone kind of saw that I was trying to get where I needed to be, and, slowly but surely, I got there. Heading in to Week 2,

Jim Harbaugh, who was the head coach of the 49ers at the time, came up to me in practice and said, "You're starting to get your legs under you. I like that." I was feeling a lot better, a lot more in game shape. But because I was so far behind in my training, I ended up tearing my meniscus in that Week 2 game against the Dallas Cowboys.

Just as I was starting to feel good, I hurt my knee. I was carrying a bit more weight than I usually did. I was probably around 226 pounds at the time and I weighed around 215 my Pro Bowl year. There was extra weight on the knee, and then Cowboys safety Abe Elam put a little weight on it in the game, and it tore. It wasn't intentional by Elam, and I think if I had been at the weight I normally was and the shape I normally was, it might not have happened anyway.

Either way, the injury happened, and there's nothing I could do but look forward. We talked to the general manager, Trent Baalke; Harbaugh; and the doctors about surgery and the next steps. Harbaugh and I had a good relationship until I got hurt. He liked the effort, the energy, and that I was balling. But when I got hurt, there was nothing to talk about, and the relationship was different. I know everyone thinks there's this big Michigan connection with us, but I didn't know much about him before I got to San Francisco. I knew what he did at Stanford, how he was able to turn that program around, and that he had Pete Carroll's number, but that was it. I liked Harbaugh, but I think he fits the college level a lot better than the NFL.

He treated NFL players like they're in college. He tried to monopolize your time, which will work for 20-year-old kids, but it doesn't work for 30-year-old men with wives and kids. When I was with Rex Ryan and Romeo Crennel, they realized that football isn't everything. Football is amazing. I love what football has allowed me to do. It allowed me to go to college for free, allowed me to travel, and allowed me to meet different people. It taught me about myself and about life, but it isn't everything. I don't think Harbaugh knew that, or he at least didn't portray it to his players. Playing a season with him is like a never-ending training camp. In training camp we would finish at 10:00 PM. I had to rush to get snacks or whatever I wanted and get back to the hotel as fast as I could in order to make it back for curfew by 11:00 PM. At other places I would have had time to go home, let my dog out, do a few things, and then go back to the hotel. He had a cot in his office, so I don't think it even bothered him to stay late like that.

Harbaugh loves football, which is a good thing, but I don't think you can operate that way in the NFL and make your whole life about football. With my injury that's why I just felt like it would be best to do what he and the team wanted. If I went with Harbaugh's plan, it would show I'm a team player. You always had an option to get a second opinion, and everyone always went to Dr. James Andrews in Alabama to get an injury requiring surgery looked at.

I was starting to get nervous about things. I was no longer the No. 3 draft pick or Pro Bowl Braylon Edwards. I was not back-to-back AFC Championship Game Braylon Edwards. I just got nervous about the whole situation and thought maybe it would be a good idea if I just used the 49ers doctors. Maybe that would show a sign of good faith and make them happy. Plus, it's the Stanford medical team that they used, and that's a great school. I thought that would be the best option, so that's what I did.

The problem with that—and the problem that I had with injuries overall—was that the doctors tell the coach when someone should be back from an injury and able to participate again.

I never thought they should do that because every injury is different, and every person is different. *How can they tell me that my knee feels better when I'm the one walking on it?*

I was pushing myself anyway because I wanted to get back. I didn't want to lose my spot and I was trying to appease the doctors and Harbaugh. The doctors told Harbaugh my knee should be ready in five to six weeks from the surgery. When that five-to-six week deadline hit, the coaches started having me run outside, run routes, do light lifting, and I could just feel it wasn't ready yet. I tore my ACL on the same leg, so I knew that knee and just knew it wasn't feeling right yet. The doctor said I should be ready to go, though, so everyone started asking what was up with the knee and why it wasn't ready. Screw the doctor; my knee said it wasn't ready.

I was in a one-year contract. So in my mind, I thought, *I need to get back and get this right. I better get back out there and play.* It just wasn't the same, though. I could see it on film after the games. I could see it and I always wondered why they couldn't. I was obviously not right, but I had to keep playing. I didn't want to lose my spot.

I pushed through it but ended up hurting my shoulder against the Washington Redskins and just couldn't get it right. As the season went on, the knee just was not getting any better. Now I was miserable because my body wasn't allowing me to do what I thought I should be able to on the field. Because of my DUI, I wasn't allowed to drink and had to do random urine tests to check if I was. I couldn't play like I wanted to, I couldn't drink, I didn't have a wife by my side to talk to, and I was far away from home without family to talk to. It's really difficult going from being what you knew you were and what people saw you were to not being able to do much of anything.

We played the Seattle Seahawks, the 49ers' big rival during those years, on Christmas Eve, and my knee was shot. I can tell now that it was a combination of a surgery that didn't go as it should have and me being rushed back to get on the field. Because of that it just wasn't healing properly. After the game was over, I was back at my house and I got a call from Baalke asking me to come into his office. I was only about 10 minutes from the facility, so I went right up to his office. I sat down with him, and he said, "Hey Braylon, the situation's just not working for us. The knee is just not responding the way we want it to."

They gave me the bullshit speech, and then he said Harbaugh wanted to talk to me on my way out. I told Baalke: fuck you and that I didn't want to go see Harbaugh. *See him for what? They rushed me back, and my knee wasn't ready. And now it's not working for them, and I get cut the day after Christmas?* Why did I need to go talk to him? What was there to talk about? I didn't talk to him; I just left and went home.

Technically, at that point, I wasn't in the NFL anymore. I went out and partied just to get my mind somewhere else. I couldn't believe that's how they ended it—before the regular season was even over. There was only one game left, and they cut me. The funny part about that was that they made the playoffs that year. I had those incentives in my contract, so I got money for them making the playoffs, even though I wasn't even on the team anymore. They made it to the NFC Championship Game against the New York Giants, and I was rooting against them because they cut me but also rooting for them because I'd keep getting more money if they won. If they would've made it to the Super Bowl, I would have gotten something like an extra $40,000. Then if they had won the Super Bowl, it would have been an extra $100,000. They lost to the Giants, though, so that money never came.

It was January 2012, and I was just on my own at this point with a bum knee and no prospects. After talking to my mom and the people around me, we decided it was time to get my knee looked at by another doctor. I decided to go back to Miami and meet with Dr. John Uribe, who was the team physician for the Miami Dolphins. I wasn't old, so I knew something was wrong and that I still had a lot left to give. We wanted to make sure there wasn't an issue with the knee structurally and that it could eventually heal. I was only 29 years old at the time, so I felt like I could get my knee right and get myself another opportunity.

Dr. Uribe took some X-Rays and did an MRI, and when the MRI came back, he said I had a shoddy surgery. I had loose bodies in my knee that needed to come out. He told me my knee wasn't healed and that he would need to go in and clean it up. Then I was even more mad because I just lost my chance with the 49ers from something that was out of my control, and then a doctor was telling me that the procedure was part of the problem. I trusted Dr. Uribe and decided to have the surgery to clean everything up in hopes that it would help me get back on track. I was already down on myself, and the thoughts were creeping up that it was going to be harder and harder for me to get back to where I wanted to be.

In the beginning of January, I went in for the surgery. At about 6:00 AM, as I'm driving to the hospital, my mom called. This wasn't an intricate or dangerous surgery, so I had a feeling something was wrong. She wasn't worried about my surgery, so why else would she be calling this early? She asked me how I was doing in a calm but nervous voice. We all know our parents, and so I could really tell by her voice that something was up.

I asked her what was happening and—before she could get it out—I asked if something had happened to my godfather, Dennis Caver. He was the closest person to me outside of any of my parents. He was always there for me, and we just had this connection that I didn't have with anyone else. At the time he was 56 and was somewhat of a father figure—as well as a friend I could confide in. During some of these ups and downs I was experiencing in the NFL, Caver was always there for me with advice or just to take my mind off of whatever I was dealing with. He used to always cheat at the game Words with Friends, too. But we loved just being around each other. That New Year's Eve, he came over to my house, and we shot pool together, so I was just with him a few days prior. We shot 20 games of pool that night. The reason I remember is because I kept winning. I was up 9–0, and he said, "Godson, I'm not letting you get to 10." Then it was 10–0, and he said I wouldn't beat him to 15. Then it was 15, and he said he'd be damned if he let me get to 20, and, sure enough, I got to 20. He said, "I'm taking my ass home. This is too much." We had just talked about how he wanted to get married and what he wanted to do with the rest of his life.

I don't know how I knew that my mom was calling about Caver that day, but I just had a sixth sense about it. She told me he had been hit by a car on the Lodge Freeway and died.

At first, while I was in the car, I was handling it well—or at least well enough. I got to the hospital, put my gown on, got prepped, and then everything hit me all at once. I asked the nurses if I could put my clothes back on and have a moment. I got dressed and found the chapel inside the hospital, went inside, and just let go. I lost it.

We were so close. This guy didn't have to love me like a son, but he did, and then he was gone. I was in Miami, away from home. I was about to go into surgery and I didn't know what's next. I got cut from a team for the first time in my life. There was so much happening all at once that I was just emotionally drained, and Caver leaving us was the final moment for me. My emotions poured out in that small chapel. Sitting in a sterile hospital by myself not knowing what was next for me, it all just left my body. I eventually gathered myself and went back to the nurses for the surgery.

The procedure went as planned, and I decided to stay in Miami for my rehab. I needed to be by myself after the news about Caver. I was already feeling a little lost with how the season ended, and this threw me into somewhat of a tailspin. I was depressed, sulking, and didn't really know what was next for me. I wanted to be by myself, but at the same time, being by myself probably wasn't the best thing for me. I always had my mom there for me when I was younger, dealing with issues this monumental, but now I was trying to figure it out on my own as a man.

Mom probably would've been able to guide me better than I was guiding myself, especially since I had run into my ex-girlfriend around February. We dated in 2008 since I was always in Miami, and she worked in the restaurant industry down there. We started hanging out again and eventually started dating again. It was a familiar face and someone I felt comfortable with, so it just kind of happened. We were out for my birthday one night, and she tried to give me some molly or ecstasy, whatever you want to call it, because she was selling it on the side. Up to this point, the only drug I had ever done was smoked a little weed. I drank, but that was it. I told myself I would always stay away from drugs, but she urged me and told me to stop worrying so much and relax.

I was depressed. I had no team to report to, I was cut, and my best friend passed away. So I was going to try this and just escape for a little bit. I tried it and I liked the way it made me feel. Molly will alter your mind and make you feel like there's nothing wrong in the world. It's an upper, and the problem with an upper is when you come down from it, the issues I was running away from came to the forefront even stronger.

My depression became more intense, so it created this cycle where I became dependent on the drug to keep me in this altered state to hide from everything that was around me. It's like it got taken from me so fast. One minute I was wearing No. 1 at Michigan, drafted No. 3 overall by the Cleveland Browns, appearing in the Pro Bowl, playing in two AFC Championships Game with a coach that you really like. Then after two years, it was just like I was not wanted.

After getting in trouble, I couldn't get the Cardinals deal. Then I got hurt, and the 49ers didn't want me. I went from sugar to shit. I went from traded to not being picked. Those are the signs of it being over. I started paying attention to those signs, and it messed with my head. Then I started running into my ex-girlfriend, who was selling uppers, and I started enjoying the masking of my real life.

Everything compounded off the DUI I got. I started asking myself if I was an embarrassment, if I wasn't good enough. Not just good enough as a football player, but am I good enough as a person? I started to question everything, and then depression took a hold of me. I started to look at all the little things in my life. *Am I going to get married? What do I do next?* I couldn't shut my mind off and then I stopped sleeping. All over television and online, I saw about concussions and wondered if I was fucked up. I didn't know if I was all right. I needed someone to lean on, and the person nearest to me was my girlfriend. She eventually moved in with me, and since she was selling uppers, I became dependent on her, which caused an even further spiral downward.

I started missing rehab sessions for my knee. I went to some of them, but if I was out partying the night before, I would skip the session and just not worry about it. Since she worked at a restaurant, I would go up to the restaurant, grab some drinks, and then go party once she got off work. It just kept going and going and it was this constant chasing away of my feelings and trying to stay a couple steps ahead from that comedown.

It got so bad that I wasn't eating right anymore. I had dropped down to about 205 pounds around May 2012. I was 226 during the season with the 49ers just a few months prior and I hadn't been 205 pounds since my sophomore year at Michigan. When you're not around family a lot or people you trust, you can kind of ignore what you see in the mirror. You can brush your teeth with your head down and hide from that mirror. But what helped wake me up is when I came into contact with people that I have known since I was in diapers. I went back home to Detroit for Mother's Day, and my grandma looked at me said, "Boy, are you eating?" It's always the grandmas who are worried about us eating, but this time she knew something was wrong and she was right. I was in this downward spiral, trying to figure everything out.

My grandma and parents had a conversation with me about what I was doing and where I was headed. The path I was on would never help me get back on an NFL roster and it just wasn't who I was. I had never done any kind of drug like that before nor run from my problems, and then there I was using something to escape and not deal with my problems. That conversation with my grandma and my parents woke me up. I realized that I'm not the self-loathing type. I had a rough patch, but we're human; we all go through that. I'd never been the guy to just throw it in and give up. I'd been through a lot as a kid, dealing with the relationship with my father and everything else I struggled through. I could deal with this too. I just needed to face it head on instead of hiding from it.

I decided I needed to get back into shape and get my body right before I could do anything else. I went back to Miami and started working out with the University of Miami's strength and conditioning coach, Andrew Swayze. We worked hard from May through June and July—to the point where I felt like I was in playing shape again. We went after it. College workouts weren't like NFL workouts, and I was working with the Miami team.

In the NFL you can take a break here and there, but you can't do that in college. They go at it, and this was Miami, so the players were hitting it hard. I told my agent I felt good and was ready to go, so he got me a tryout with the Dolphins and the Seahawks. I worked out for the Dolphins and thought I killed the workout but didn't get a decision either way. About a day later, I jumped on a plane and went out to Seattle for my workout with the Seahawks. They had Antonio Bryant, who I knew from back when I was in college and from the Browns, and me out on the same day. We worked out and killed that one, too.

Unfortunately, there was still no clarity. Just the same as Miami, the Seahawks didn't give me a yes or no. I was in a better state of mind at this point where I had gotten my hopes back up, gotten my body right, and knew that I did everything I needed in the workout. I figured that even if the Dolphins or Seahawks didn't pick me up, my knee was finally right, my body was in good shape, and if worst came to worst, I could always call old coaches I've played for and tell them I'm healthy.

I flew back to Miami and was at a pool party when I got a call from my agent. He said the Seahawks were upset that I left because they wanted to sign me to a contract. This was toward the end of July, so we only had a few days until training camp. I was ready to go physically, but I wanted to get out to Seattle as soon as possible to get with the team and sign the contract.

At this time I was still with my girlfriend, but I stopped taking molly when I started working out with Swayze back in June or July. I knew if I was going to get myself right that I needed to stop taking it. She flew out to Seattle with me for that first day and stayed in the hotel for two more after that. I flew her back home and called my mom. This girl wasn't the best look for me since she was selling ecstasy, and I was trying to get back on the straight and narrow. My mom said, "Listen, you have a new team, new situation, new chance, I don't think..." She didn't even have to finish the sentence. I already knew what she was going to say and I said, "I agree." When my girlfriend landed back in Miami, I called her and told her it wasn't going to work out for me anymore, and we cut ties.

I cut ties with that period in my life and luckily had the support system to realize I needed to pick myself up before it got too out of control. I had a new opportunity in front of me and I needed to make the most of it. I had already seen signs that my career could be coming to an end, so this was something I was taking very seriously.

After going through training camp and making my mark, I ended up starting on Opening Day. Golden Tate was hurt in the last preseason game, and I had a great camp, so the coaches told me I earned it, and Doug Baldwin and myself were the starters. It was rejuvenating to hear a coach call me a starter again. No matter what has happened throughout my career, I earned the starting job when the season began. The fact that I was always a starter, no matter where I was, motivated me. It made me proud that I had dealt with the death of Caver, my release from the 49ers, surgery, drug addiction, and now I had everything in front of me once again. It was gratification and it felt great.

That feeling only lasted a short amount of time, though. When Week 2 rolled around, I was no longer the starter. Carroll doesn't like older players. He likes you when you're in Year One to Year Seven, and then it starts to go downhill with him. I went from starter to only getting about 10 to 12 snaps a game. Tate was back from injury, but I was killing it at practice. We had something called practice cam, where we would watch all the highlights from practice the day before. During every practice cam, I was on there two or three times, making a crazy catch, crazy block, or blowing by the coverage.

As the season went on, I started to see Jermaine Kearse work his way into my spot. Then Father Time started to work against me, and I was icing my knees more and more each week. I didn't let it hinder me, though, and I was destroying the Legion of Boom in practice. We played the New England Patriots during the season and I scored my 40th touchdown, which would wind up being my last NFL touchdown ever. The Seahawks started giving me more plays in that game, featuring me in the red zone.

And then we played the Lions at Detroit. I worked hard to get to this point, basically had to eat humble pie and take my lumps without playing much. I had the issue with my knee, but instead of getting upset, I just put my head down and went to work. I hustled, grinded, and it started to pay off leading up to that Lions game. I was excited, but I also knew that all that work was putting a toll on my knee. In practice the week before the game, I took a shot in my knee to help with the pain. That helped me feel good, so I started working it even harder. I was doing one-on-ones, going back-to-back and was excited because I was going back home to play in Detroit.

I didn't realize it until Friday when we were on the plane to fly to Detroit for the game that I had worked my knee way too hard. Halfway through the flight, I could feel my knee swelling up through my suit. I was icing it on the plane and at the hotel. I was nervous because I could just tell that my knee wasn't going to be able to go on Sunday, but I didn't say anything to anyone. Gameday came, and my knee looked like a balloon.

The trainers and doctors had to draw blood out of it to see if I could even warm up. I went on the field, but I knew immediately I wouldn't be able to go. I missed the game and went back to Seattle to get my knee right. The doctors gave me a cortisone shot back in Seattle, and everything started to go back to normal, and the swelling went away.

I could still tell that the knee wasn't going to hold up forever, but I could at least play and felt like I could contribute. We eventually played the Bears in Chicago and I scored a touchdown at the end of the half. The refs reviewed it, though, and said I didn't get my hands under it. I was pissed because I knew I had my arms underneath it, but they didn't give me the touchdown. We ended up going to overtime, and I pulled my hamstring earlier in the game, which sidelined me.

I took a muscle relaxer once we were on the plane and headed back to Seattle. I was already angry about the touchdown called back and then I became angry that I pulled my hamstring. All players drink on the plane ride home, especially if you're going from Chicago to Seattle after a good win. I poured myself a drink and I didn't even think that I was mixing alcohol with a muscle relaxer.

During the game the strength and conditioning coach came up to me and told me I needed to get my hands underneath the ball to make that play. Then he did it again on the plane, telling me I needed to put my body on the line and make the play. This was the strength and conditioning coach; that's not his fucking job to tell me this. One, I caught the ball. Two, this was not the weight room. Then during the game they threw me a post route, and I had Charles Tillman beat. Russell Wilson hung one up there. He threw a pop fly, so I had to come back to get the ball. That gave Tillman time to catch up and make a play, and he swatted the ball away. The strength coach then told me on the plane that I needed to make that play for Wilson and that we might not go to overtime if I made that play.

The alcohol and muscle relaxer were starting to kick in now, so I just looked at him like, *what the hell are you talking about?* Between me being mad about my snaps and my hamstring, I had enough. I was feeling myself and I got on the public-address system at the back of the plane and just started cracking jokes, poking fun at everyone. I was cracking jokes on the strength coach, Carroll, everyone. Everybody was dying laughing. I thought everyone was having a good time, but I found out the next day that wasn't the case.

I got called in to the facilities and told that Coach Carroll wanted to talk to me. They told me the whole thing on the plane wasn't a good look for the franchise. I said, "All I did was bust my ass for you, get shot up with cortisone, put everything on the line, and you can't take a joke?" They told me right there that they were parting ways and that I was cut.

I was cut again, and this time there were only four games left in the season. I was older and I knew that I was running out of time. My old friend—uncertainty—was starting to creep in again.

A New Path

I WAS UPSET THAT I WAS CUT FROM ANOTHER TEAM, BUT GETTING cut this time was different than getting cut from the San Francisco 49ers. The uncertainty I had this time around wasn't so much about whether another team would pick me up. It was now about whether or not my career was over. I was starting to feel the bumps and bruises throughout the season and could tell my body wasn't taking to the constant pounding.

I was cut by the Seattle Seahawks on December 4, two days after the Chicago Bears game, but I had no idea at the time that a tweet from a few weeks prior would help me land my next job. On November 22 the New York Jets were playing the New England Patriots, and Mark Sanchez ran the ball into the back of his offensive lineman, which caused a fumble—the infamous butt fumble. Everyone was on Sanchez about that play, calling him out for running into your own lineman and losing the ball.

I felt like I needed to stick up for him, so I tweeted out that it wasn't Sanchez's fault. It was the fault of general manager Mike Tannenbaum, who got rid of all his playmakers and helped cause something like that. Sanchez called me after that and said he appreciated it and was glad I had his back. I ended up issuing an apology for the tweet, but it was true. After that game against the Patriots, the Jets were 4–7 and limping through the season. Once I was cut, I think the Jets organization knew they needed a familiar face around, someone who could help excite the fans because I still had a lot of love for and from the New York fans. I didn't leave on bad terms there, so those fans were still behind me. My agent called me and asked how I'd like to go back to New York, and I said, "Let's do it."

When they thought about winning, they thought about our AFC Championship Game teams. Even though I was critical in my tweet, I apologized and I still believe that tweet had something to do with me coming back to New York. At this point the Jets were 6–7, but I was still nervous because I wasn't in the same health as I was during those playoff years. I didn't want to let the fans down because they were so good to me. I was still dealing with the hamstring injury, but it felt a lot better to where I thought I could go on it. The knee wasn't hindering me from playing, but it was still hurting from the wear and tear of the season.

Plus, on top of the injuries I was dealing with, my first game back with the Jets was on *Monday Night Football*. I don't know what it is about me and Monday night in New York, but that always seemed to be my first stage during my Jets years. We played the Tennessee Titans this time, and I could tell right away I was going to have problems. I had two big catches, but I was having trouble getting out of the gate. I felt like I was a slow receiver or a thin tight end because I wasn't moving very fast.

I was excited to be back in New York, but at the same time I noticed the energy was so different from the last time I was there. We went into halftime down four points, so we were still in the game. You wouldn't have known that from the way the guys were acting in the locker room, though. The spirit in the locker room was like: here we go again. They had gone through a string of losing, so they started to fall into that trap, thinking it was going to happen again.

I got up and yelled in the locker room, asking them what was wrong with them. I let them know the butt fumble was three weeks ago. We needed to get in this game and win it. The talk didn't work, though, and we lost to the Titans.

We lost to the San Diego Chargers the next week, and it just seemed like nobody wanted it anymore. The older guys had checked out. It was different than the way guys acted in Cleveland, though. When I was with the Browns, it had the vibe of: all right, we suck. In New York we had a taste of being good, and then it was more depressing to everyone that we were in this position.

We ended up finishing that season 6–10, losing the last three games of the year. The season ended, and I went back to wondering if I could go another round and if a team would take a chance on me. Once again, feelings of the unknown and asking myself if I was good enough started to make their way into my head. Football was able to help me push those thoughts away, but when it was taken away from me, those thoughts snuck back in and took over.

I went back to Miami for the offseason, and you can probably guess what happened. I was back partying, doing molly, and trying to mask the fact that this could be the end of my football career. The difference this time around was that I stayed in shape the whole offseason. I went back to working out with Andrew Swayze at Miami and was ripped the whole time. But I was back in the adult playground, running from the fact that I didn't know what was next for me. I waited through January, February, March, April, and there were still no calls. Then May, June, and finally as the end of July rolled around, the Jets were back on the phone. They said, "Braylon, are you ready to come to training camp?"

I thought: *What took so long*. But I wasn't about to turn down an NFL job. Since I had been working out the whole time, I was up to 217 pounds and already in playing shape, but I was worried about my knee. I passed a running test with the knee, but I could tell the knee wasn't going to hold up. I could run straight, but I had trouble with the cuts. I got through training camp and felt all right, and then we played the Jacksonville Jaguars in the third preseason game, and I tore some ligaments in my ankle. It just wasn't healing or getting better, so they cut me right before the last preseason game.

Initially, when I was cut, I went back to Miami because it was always my safe place. But I knew I couldn't keep going through this cycle, so after a week or two, I went back home to Detroit. At this point, I knew it was the end. I knew that my body couldn't hold up anymore, and it just wasn't going to happen. The problem was that I needed to keep up the façade for friends and family that I was still going to give it another shot and that I still believed I could make a team. I went from the No. 1 jersey, No. 3 pick, a Pro Bowl, two AFC Championship Games, to getting cut and having injuries.

I decided that I would start working out with my dad, Stan, again. Regardless of our bumps and bruises, I know who got me here. I'll never take credit away from him for that. I was the guinea pig back in high school for my dad's training regimen, but by this time, he had perfected the program on my younger brother, Berkley. He turned Berkley into one of the fastest kids in the country, and Berkley was a freak.

It goes back to my love for *Rocky*. It was like in *Rocky III* when Apollo Creed told Rocky he needed to go back to the basics and get back to what got him here in the first place. That was my dad for me. I went in the garage with my dad, and we got after it. The difference between this time and the first time was that I was the one pushing it now. I was the one who was dialing it up and asking for more. I started lifting weights with him, and it felt good. Not just to be with him, but the weightlifting was giving me a new high. I never took any supplements while I was playing, but I started to take some pre-workout, muscle mass, and other over-the-counter products and I was loving the results I was getting.

The only thing was that my knee just never felt like it was 100 percent. I was cautious with how I was moving while running, but we hit the weights hard. Working out with my dad felt good, but he was also the one person I knew I couldn't cheat. You can cheat an NFL strength coach or someone you're paying, but you can't do that with your dad. He knows if you're bullshitting. That time spent together actually brought us closer, which was a bit funny because it caused us to drift apart the first time around. My whole life was starting to come back full circle but shift in a new, positive but opposite way. We had gotten away from each other from about 2010 until this time in 2013. We lost our connection, and this helped us get that back.

The only problem that came with it was that working out eventually became my addiction. It replaced the drugs and it gave me an outlet to channel my frustration. When you're not going to practice or on a team, you start to miss those little things. You miss the camaraderie, the jokes. You miss being on the same schedule every day.

I had been on a similar schedule from 18 years old to 30. For 12 years I was essentially doing the same thing every day and then in an instant I was sitting at home watching games on TV. That was hard to deal with and difficult to adjust to. When football was such a big part of my life, it was shocking to have it gone in an instant. It's like being forced to retire from your job at 31 years old, shoved out the door with no help, and then I was supposed to just find a new career.

You use vices to mask stuff. Similar to what I did with the ecstasy before my Seattle days, my new vice was working out and sleeping. Working out was a healthy life, but I was taking it to an extreme. My schedule was meal prepping at 7:00 AM, drinking a protein shake right out of the gate, making breakfast, doing cardio, showering, more meal prepping and more eating, drinking a protein shake, preparing lunch, lifting weights, eating again, meal prepping for my dinner, doing an ab circuit at the end of the night, and then drinking one last protein shake. I took it over the top with how big I got and how much I was putting myself through in the weight room. I was 224 pounds with around 5 percent body fat, which was big for me back then.

In between meal prepping and working out, I was watching some of the NFL games on TV just to see what was going on. That made sitting at home even worse because I knew I was better than some of those guys I was watching. That made me even more angry that I couldn't get a shot, so then I started working out even more and pushing myself even harder just to take my mind away from the game.

Once that 2013 season was over, I hadn't played and I didn't have any interest coming in from teams, so I decided to hire a new agent, Neil Schwartz. He was a little more hands-on with his clients in terms of working for the client and going out and trying to help create opportunities. Tom Condon was an amazing agent, but when your client's last name was Manning, you didn't have to do a whole lot of work. If you're representing Joe Blow or a guy who is trying to get back in the league, you have to grind and stay on the phone.

In January of 2014, I moved back to Miami to train with Swayze. This time I was not into the party scene or doing drugs. I was just there to work out and see if any teams might have any interest. We got through spring and into summer, and I could tell teams just weren't checking in anymore. I knew it was over. In June I called Schwartz and told him to stop looking for a new team. I told him I was good. It was time to stop trying to use a vice to mask reality. It was time to look in that mirror and understand that my football career was over.

To say that I was done still hurts because I still believed there was so much left on the table. I started hitting my stride during my Pro Bowl year in 2007 and then the two years in New York. I was moving in a forward direction, and then all of the sudden, the lockout hit. Then I got injured and cut. To hang it up then sucked. When people ask me why I retired, it's the question I hate the most. I understand why they ask, but it still hurts.

I thought I would end my career with the Jets. I loved the fans, I loved Rex Ryan, the two AFC Championship Games. I was part of that. It's cliché, but now as I look back on it, I'm not mad that it happened; I'm happy that I was a part of it. At the time I was mad, but now I'm a little older and wiser, and it's easier to separate myself from the emotions to realize that I was part of a great thing and that I should cherish that part of it.

When I told Schwartz to stop looking, I didn't tell my family about that conversation. But somehow my mom knew that it was over and told me it was time to come back to Detroit. I fought her on it and said I wanted to stay in Miami, but she told me I needed to come home to refocus. She made a good point about where I should be by asking me where my biggest fanbase was. I said Ann Arbor. She said that's 30 minutes from Detroit. Once again, she was right, and I decided to go home.

Now my life became thinking about how to do a complete 180 professionally and what I could get into. Football wasn't always everything to me, but it was the biggest aspect of my life for as long as I could remember. Now that's gone, and I had to figure out what I could do and what I was capable of doing. Everyone always told me I spoke well and that I would be good on TV, but I didn't want to do what everyone else was doing and just go straight from the field to the studio. I mulled that over for a while until I happened to run into a local sportscaster, Don Shane, at a restaurant in August. I've known Shane since I was a kid because he was around my dad and around the Michigan program. He was the nicest guy. When I ran into him at the restaurant, I told him I retired, and he asked if I would be up for doing some work with Channel 7 news, the ABC station he had been affiliated with for many years.

He told me he thought I would be good on TV. In 2008 I had appeared on Bob Costas' HBO show with Buzz Bissinger and Will Leitch, which discussed the role of sports blogs. The episode went viral, but it was a weird experience. I didn't get to talk a lot and wasn't sure why I was involved in the conversation. It was more about Bissinger vs. Leitch.

Anyhow, after I spoke with Shane, the wheels started spinning in my head. I thought maybe if I could get my feet wet with Channel 7, then I could turn that into something else. I started doing a few shows with them and getting a feel for talking about the game and actually saying what I wanted to say. This was the first time that I could give my opinion or what I wanted to say without any backlash from coaches or players.

When I played for the Browns and you asked me about Brady Quinn, I wanted to tell you he threw knuckleballs in the dirt, but I couldn't tell you that. Now I could say whatever I wanted within reason. This was something I started to really have fun with, and in late 2014, someone from IMG reached out to me about representing me for a potential TV career. We started working together, and I started getting gigs with ESPN, FOX, and CBS, and it started becoming more and more exciting. I got to do a little more than just football, too, which is what I wanted. I love football, but I'm not like some of these old heads who need to be directly involved with football at all times to fill that void. Since I ran track throughout high school and college, I was doing some track meets for the Pac-12 Network.

In May of 2015, I did a track meet in Arizona and then went out that night with some friends in Old Town Scottsdale. We were at my cousin's house, his Wi-Fi wasn't working to get the Uber to come get us, so I just decided to drive. We went out, stopped at a few places, and then finished the night at a pizza place. Everyone was ready to leave so I decided to drive my cousin's car home. I was used to my car that has automatic headlights and didn't realize that you had to turn his car's on.

I made a left near the W Hotel, made a left by the Scottsdale Fashion Square, and got pulled over for not having my headlights on. The police officer came up to the car, and I apologized for not having my lights on and explained the situation. He asked me if I had been drinking and I said I had a few earlier, but the last hour or so we were just chilling, eating pizza.

They were very nice cops, but they gave me all the field sobriety tests, and I passed those. He asked me to count backward, touch my nose, walk the line, and I did all of that. Then he said, "The last one I'm going to ask you to do is..."

I interrupted him and said just take me to jail. I knew he was going to give me a breathalyzer. He asked if I was sure because refusing a breathalyzer is the same as failing one.

We started early that day, so I knew I would fail it. Oddly enough, he was a Michigan fan and knew who I was. He had to do his job, though, and took me to jail. The Maricopa County Court system acts very quickly with getting paperwork filed to obtain bloodwork and urine samples, so I was only in the tank for about 30 minutes before they took my blood and urine. I paid a fine, and they let me go.

I wasn't too worried because I figured I had been out of football for a while, and so it wouldn't be a big media story. About a week went by, and nothing hit the news, so I thought I was good. There was nothing Monday, but on Tuesday I was traveling to Chicago, and right as I got to the airport at 9:00 AM, TMZ went public with it and posted that I got my second DUI.

I got a call from my agent at IMG almost immediately. He was upset that I didn't tell him about it and felt that I should be sharing everything with him. I told him I didn't think there was anything to share, but he said they represented me, and they should know everything. They said that wasn't how they operated and so could no longer work with me. They dropped me.

The Pac-12 Network was mad at my agent because my agent didn't tell them about it, which I understood. Because I didn't disclose it, they allowed someone on the air who just got a DUI. I completely understood their perspective, but they let me go as well. They say history repeats itself, and for me it certainly did. These were different parameters in a different environment, but in a way, I was cut again and potentially putting my new career in jeopardy because of a bad decision.

Because this was my second DUI, I was put on house arrest and had to stay at home. That made me restless, and I decided to start weightlifting again to pass the time and take my mind off of everything around me. But this time I wound up breaking my hand while lifting. I basically got cut from an organization and then injured. Does that sound familiar? This injury was probably a blessing, though. It made me stop lifting altogether and helped me get my mind better and realize that I didn't need to lift weights to fill any voids. I could live a normal life and not have these obsessive addictions to get me through anything.

I was still exercising and working out, but I had gotten myself all the way up to 252 pounds with around 5 percent body fat at one point. I wasn't drinking because I had to be tested four times a day with the home detention, so I was lean but huge. It looked incredible, but it felt awkward on me that I was carrying that much weight. Once I broke my hand, I dropped down to 230, and that weight felt a lot better.

Breaking my hand kicked me into gear and made me realize that I could still become a sports broadcaster. One mistake didn't kill my dream in the NFL, and if I really wanted this, I needed to learn from my past and figure this out. On April of 2016, I decided to go to broadcast boot camp to try to hone my skills and make some connections in the industry. It was the NFL Network boot camp, but every broadcast channel was there, including FOX, NBC, Big Ten Network, etc. I realized after that boot camp that I needed to stay on the straight and narrow. This wasn't college anymore or playing in the league. This was me being a man and having a professional career that I needed to take seriously. I needed to go by the book and be straitlaced. I had to be a new me.

As you could probably guess, my mom was behind me getting on the straight and narrow, too. She told me that she'll always be there for me, but she couldn't hold my hand through every process. She can't walk me through everything. At some point I had to take control. I had to want it myself, and that became her message. If you're on home detention and living with your mom, you couldn't hide from her. So she was on me, but I needed it and started going to work.

I got a few gigs here and there, but there wasn't really anything steady coming in. I was still in a good state of mind, but I really didn't know what I should be doing next. I wasn't familiar with this industry or how it worked. And because of my DUI, I still didn't have an agent representing me or helping me. But by happenstance, Michigan had hired Warde Manuel as its new athletic director in January of 2016.

My life was coming full circle once again while also pushing it in a new, positive direction. Manuel was a big part of my college experience when he was an associate athletic director. He was always there for me with advice. He was someone I could talk to and became an important piece of my time at Michigan. When I couldn't figure out what my next move should be, I knew I needed to go talk to Manuel.

I never knew what Part II was for me. Part I was supposed to be this amazing football career, and would Part II just fall in my lap, where I'd do some commercials or cheesy shit to make money? I told Manuel that, even though I heard it throughout my college career, I never really thought that I would need to focus on anything but football. He looked at me and asked me if I had ever finished my degree at Michigan, which I hadn't. He said, "Let's start there. Why don't you finish your degree, make some friends, and I'll have you out at some events where you can rub elbows and figure out where you want to go?"

Manuel gave me some great advice in that meeting. He's a sharp brother. He's smooth and he has been through it all. He had a football career that didn't go the way he wanted, but he found another path, so he was the perfect person for me to talk to.

As bad as this sounds, when guys get hurt in college, I think it's an advantage for them in terms of figuring out their Part II. They know they're not going to the NFL, so they realize at the time that they need to make the most out of their college experience and education. If you get hurt in the NFL, it happens late enough that you haven't thought that far ahead.

Thanks to Manuel, I went back to school to finish my degree. And because I did that and because my mom helped me get on a straight path, I wound up making some connections with the Big Ten Network and working for them as an analyst. I went in to the Chicago studio on Thursday or Friday, and we broke down what we expected from the coaching, player substitutions, etc. from the weekend games. The show I did in 2017 just covered the Big Ten. Everything was going well. It was supposed to go through the Big Ten championship, which was Wisconsin-Ohio State. They asked me to come back through the rest of December, through bowl season, through January, and going through the signing period. Then they extended my contract after that season, and in 2018 I was doing the big show that covers the top 25 and covered the top programs nationally, too. Their idea was to give me more to do this time. It was kind of the pulse of NCAA football vs. the Big Ten. I did some halftime shows, gave my analysis, and outlined what I expected during the second half. I was also going to do some sideline reporting and things of that nature. That's where I was going, so I thought it was a good stepping-stone. It's a good place to hone your skills, and there are some good people there. It's a great place to make the next step in my career.

The night of the Michigan-Notre Dame game, I was at an event at Soaring Eagle in Mount Pleasant, Michigan. We were at a Michigan event, and a lot of former Michigan players came to it, including Rick Leach, Ron Bellamy, Dave Terrell, and my father. It was a good mix of former players from different eras. It gave fans a chance to shoot the breeze, have a couple drinks, and talk about the state of Michigan football. And it gave us players a chance to catch up, too.

We were having a good time and we started talking about what we had seen from the program since Jim Harbaugh's been there. It always starts the same conversation about what needs to change, what can be done better. That carried into the game and the expectations of this new Michigan. It's basically just bar talk. After getting some drinks, passion got mixed in. Emotions were high. We wanted to see Michigan move forward and prove itself with this new team. We were struggling, not looking the part. That bar talk led to a tweet, where I criticized the offense and Cesar Ruiz and Shea Patterson. Any student watching that game at the Brown Jug or Blue Leprechaun was thinking the same thing. However, it's different when you hear someone like me say it. So once I hit send on the tweet, I caught backlash like you couldn't imagine.

That night I didn't really pay attention to it. I sent the first one and then I think I sent two and I deleted them. Then I sent a third one and didn't delete that. I didn't check Twitter that night. My friends and I went to the casino, gambled a little bit, and then I went to bed. It wasn't until the next day that I actually saw the backlash. I got a call from an executive at the Big Ten Network on Sunday, telling me to take the tweet down and that it wasn't appropriate. I deleted it and I saw what fans were saying. That was it until Harbaugh discussed it on that Monday.

I don't regret the tweet in the sense of the overall message. Look what happened at the end of the year with Ohio State and Florida. The part of the tweet that I looked at and wish I could change is talking about the players individually. I've been in those situations before where people have said things about me. Twitter wasn't around when I dropped a fourth-down pass at Ohio State. It was a case of truth vs. opinion. You should keep opinions to yourself, especially about young players.

So I definitely wish I could take that back and just tweeted the vanilla message that Michigan needs to get better, but that didn't happen. On the Big Ten Network, you can't say those things and then potentially interview these players or coaches. So that's a warning or a lesson to learn because nothing had ever happened between me and the network. This wasn't thing No. 2 or 3; this was the first issue.

When Harbaugh addressed my tweet personally, it was to the point of: don't go after my players; go after me. Big Ten Network had to look at whether this was recoverable and whether it could move forward with me. I got a call from Quentin Carter, a senior producer for the Big Ten Network. He puts people on the shows and makes personnel decisions. He called me and told me that I couldn't come in that week. It started off as just a deal for that week.

Then I had a meeting with Big Ten Network and FOX. I never received a phone call back after that. I sent out a tweet apologizing to Ruiz and Patterson, but I still stood by my overall statement about Michigan. My statement came from a place of passion. I was a kid who went to the Michigan game in 1993, where Colorado quarterback Kordell Stewart threw a Hail

Mary to win the game. We lost, and I cried. My father went to Michigan, and my brother, Berkley, is at Michigan. My uncle went there, too. Berkley had a moment this year where he was lying on Michigan's field. I'm Michigan through and through. I donate to the school.

I have always loved Michigan. It's nothing but a place of passion. You know how much money I've lost on Michigan betting when I was in the NFL? They started calling it a sucker's bet because I kept doing it. I lost a ton of money on the game in 2006 when Michigan was No. 2 and Ohio State was No. 1 because Michigan lost. I go back to Michigan, I care about the kids. For me, it's not a place of hate. It's a place of love. But I see this consistent theme. Michigan lost to Iowa in 2016 and blew its chance. The Wolverines may have stopped J.T. Barrett short, but what happened on third and long where Curtis Samuel ran the ball for nine yards? What about losing to Michigan State consistently? Look at the bowl game against Florida and against South Carolina. Every time the eyes are on, we get this different version of Michigan, and it's depressing. We're just not at that highest level and we haven't been for a long time. I regret throwing the kids in there, but I don't regret being an alum and a fan and saying we can't win in key moments. I didn't mean any harm; it wasn't malicious. Everybody makes mistakes. I still support Michigan, I'm still die-hard Michigan. I wore my Michigan jogging suit while writing this book.

I didn't call Patterson or Ruiz personally because I just wanted them to play their season out and I think enough had happened. I wanted to run into them organically. I didn't want it to be forced or that I was saying it just to save face. I reached out to Berkley and told him to tell them I was sorry, and when we see each other, there will be a conversation.

I found out that I was suspended from the Big Ten Network by seeing it on TV. The network felt it needed to cover its butt. So I was let go. The network views the players as kids. I think that's the opinion because we never had a full conversation about a specific policy or what was happening with my job. I still have not talked to anybody about what happened or the thought process of why I was let go. I wasn't a full timer. I was an independent contractor working once a week. I could work for anybody as long as it didn't interfere with the Big Ten job. So maybe they didn't think they needed to notify me; I'm not sure.

This was a chance for them to stand behind their talent. But I have no ill will toward the Big Ten Network. Carter is a good dude, and there are a lot of good people at the Big Ten Network. I think it would've been a short stay for me anyway because it's too small.

I want to move to the NFL and be an analyst with the league. I want to sit back and observe first, but I want to do something where I can speak freely. At the end of the day, I want to be able to be raw and uncut. I don't want to be held back. I'm going to sit back and observe and see what I should do next.

The only thing that had me down was the relationship with the Michigan fans. The issues that came up with the great Michigan fandom were from two kinds of people: the kids, who don't really know me or my game, were upset. Their idea of a Michigan receiver is Amara Darboh, and they don't think of me when they think Michigan receiver. The other upset ones were the fans who were distracted from the hurt of the Notre Dame loss. Upset about the loss, they put some of their anger toward me. But that was the only thing that kept me down: the fact that the relationship with the fans was hurt. I want them to know it came from passion and love and not hate. I love Michigan and the fans.

For me and my life, everything came back to where it started. My dad came back in a positive way, my mom had my best interest at hand, and Michigan became a launching point for a career. Even the conference that gave me my first shot was now giving me another chance. That's why I say: when I look back at this story, at this life, I wouldn't change a thing.

I've also found a cause that really speaks to me. In April of 2018, the NFL Alumni's Detroit chapter had different events. Their golf outings, Microsoft events, and draft parties were attached to a foundation, and they asked current or former NFL players, especially from the Detroit Lions, if they could help out. They also asked if I would participate in an impact luncheon, which was discussing the opioid epidemic taking place in Michigan. Sadly, there's a pipeline in the state, and kids are getting into it earlier and earlier. It's not just heroin and meth but pills, too. Having played in the NFL, I can relate to everyone using pills for pain and getting addicted. I had knee surgery and used pills for a little while. I saw how easy it was to use them and get hooked on them. I saw former teammates or people who didn't necessarily make it. If you get an injury, the team just gave you a bottle of pills. A lot of times those guys didn't get a second chance in the league. And if they got a second chance, they weren't as healthy as they were before, so they started depending on those pills.

I went to the luncheon and spoke with former Lions safety Ron Rice, former Lions offensive lineman Lomas Brown, and a few other people. I gave my spiel. It was a diverse group. They bussed in high school kids, and there were adults, patients, and addicts in the audience. I gave the message that addiction has no face. The people that put on the luncheon asked if I wanted to continue working with them, so I went around to a bunch of addiction centers. There was a center in Flint. We spoke with the people there and saw what they do and how they went through the process. A couple of weeks later, we went to the east side of Detroit, where the Wellness group, which is one of the main rehab and addiction centers in Michigan, is located.

I was going around—and the more and more I went to the addiction centers and talked with the patients and addicts—I realized this was something I wanted to be a part of. So I started helping with the message. It changed from me being behind the scenes to me being a more direct part of it. I talk to kids we see in high schools, middle schools, and give a relatable message. I'm crafting the message, and it's getting better and better. The first one was the typical say-no-to-drugs message that it ruins your life, but then I started to get deeper with it. I talked about the culture that's created through music, entertainment, and peer pressure. I've seen it at all levels and I've tried to make the message relatable to the kids. The ultimate message to addicts and patients is: we all fall off the bike, but you have to get up. Once you fall off, you can't lay on the concrete for too long.

We went all over the state, learning about it, falling in love with the idea of creating change and helping others. I was talking with one of my uncles, and he told me that once you stop chasing money and the cars, this lifestyle, this stereotypical success. Once you stop chasing that and start chasing passion, love, and giving back, everything else flows like it's supposed to. The best thing of 2019 so far is working with them.

Life happens, and I've definitely made mistakes, but I've grown and learned along the way. I wouldn't change that. I responded to the adversity that came my way. While I hit some bumps, I always pulled myself up with the people around me. I never would have gotten as far as I did without the people around me and I'm forever grateful for that. Those people stuck by me even when I put myself in bad situations. It seemed as though every time I put myself in a good situation that I'd take a step back. I can't change that now and I've drawn criticism along the way, but I always did it my way. I lived my life the way I wanted, and while it wasn't a straight path to where I am now, those lessons and forks in the road have helped construct the man that I am today.

Acknowledgments

I NEED TO START OUT BY THANKING MY MOM, DAD, STEPDAD, stepmom, Jade, Berkley, Brooklyn, Bailey. Grandma Shirley, Grandma Mary, Grandma, and Grandpa Plater have always been a big part of my life as well.

I have to thank Amani, Marcus, Uncle Walter, Uncle Chucky, Auntie Neicy, Auntie Angie, my cousin Jakarte, and Uncle Ricardo. Uncle Chixo and Den Daddy-O played a huge part in my life. He was always there for me with advice and a guiding voice when I needed it.

Thank you to cousin Derek Kearney, Brandon Kearney, and everyone else that has had my back.

My family has always been there for me, and I wouldn't be where I am today without them. By reading this book, you can tell that my mom has been my driving force in my life, and without her there would be no Braylon Edwards.

My dad and I have had a unique relationship, but we always come back to each other, and his role in my life is important and close to me as well.

These people have always stuck by my side through the ups and downs, and every time I fell, they were there to pick me up. Going through the journey that I have, I know how lucky I am to have such good people around me.

It's easy to be surrounded by a circle that doesn't have your best interests at heart or is there just for the ride. But my circle, my family, has always been there to uplift me and encourage me. For that, I will always be grateful.

There were some great people in my life at Michigan, people who still play an important role today. They helped shape who I am and helped mold a young, cocky kid into a man.

Warde Manuel, Greg Hardin, Coach Carr, Soup, Coach Hoke, Coach Malone, and Coach Loeffler are on that list. Shari Acho, Steve Conley, Ron Bellamy, Tyrece Butler, Marlin Jackson, David Underwood, Mike Hart, Morgan Trent, Hayes Grooms, Q Ward, Nick Beam, Key, Larnell, and Ray Hines are in there, too.

My track coaches, Fred LaPlante and Ron Warhurst. And I definitely couldn't forget the late George Sahadi, a high school coach who meant so much to me and other men that came through his doors.

My first agent, Lamont Smith, Sherard Rogers, Justin Jarvis, Tatiana Grant, and Eleanor Josaitis, who have all been good friends to me as well.

Thank you to everyone who played a part in my life, whether it was big or small, you all helped shape me into who I am today. Even if you were just in the shadows and didn't get any credit, you played a role in me pushing forward in my life.

—Braylon Edwards

I would like to thank Braylon and his family for allowing me to come in and be a part of this process and journey. When I was first approached about this project, I had a lot of questions, and after sitting down with Braylon and his family, it was clear to me that this was going to be an emotional ride with a story that had never been told.

Braylon shared some of the closest aspects of his life and memories, and to be trusted with those stories was very humbling.

I took that very seriously and I'm excited that people will be able to see behind the curtain and get a glimpse of who he is as a person, rather than just an athlete.

I'd like to thank my wife and kids as well for having the patience and understanding to allow me to complete a project of this magnitude. Showing them my work and seeing their pride is something that can't be replaced and something I cherish.

—Tom VanHaaren